JESUS
IN PRISON

Jesus in Prison

Thomas Trock

3

To my Lord and Savior Jesus Christ.

And to Jenny: God's precious gift to me.

A capable, intelligent, and virtuous woman—who is he who
can find her? She is far more precious than jewels and her
value is far above rubies or pearls

(Proverbs 31:10 AMP).

CONTENTS

FOREWORD

My name is Dr. Sammy Simpson and I am Co-founder and CEO of Global Outreach International. Since 1964, I've worked with numerous full-time Christian missionaries in nearly forty countries around the world. Although diverse in background and experiences, these missionaries share a common desire to share the saving and healing power of Jesus Christ with a lost and hurting world.

I have known Thomas Trock since 1992 and his wife Jenny since the mid-1970s. Over the years, they have been on mission trips together and worked with Global Outreach missionaries in Belize, Costa Rica, Haiti, and Kenya, East Africa. Thomas is not a pastor or a member of the clergy. He and Jenny are "regular people" whose desire is simply to tell others of Jesus.

Jesus in Prison is a book of gripping, true stories of the power of God in a place most of us seldom venture. I believe you will find these stories both compelling and challenging regardless of your background or walk in life. The chapters you are about to read embrace issues facing not only prisoners inside of institutions, but real-life, shake-you-to-the-core issues that can affect each of us or someone we know. The power of the gospel of Jesus Christ demonstrated by these events makes for compelling reading and, more importantly, illustrates that Jesus Christ truly is the answer to our deepest needs.

DR. SAMMY SIMPSON, CEO
GLOBAL OUTREACH INTERNATIONAL
TUPELO, MISSISSIPPI

PREFACE

Often when I tell people about some of the things God is doing inside the prison, they stare at me and their eyes grow wide. Sometimes they interrupt me with "No kidding?" or "That's amazing!" But perhaps the reaction I most often receive is "You need to tell people about this. You really do." This book is my humble attempt to do just that.

Many years ago when I first began going into prison to help with Bible studies, a very self-assured inmate involved in the occult confronted me. Out of the four volunteers present that night, I happened to be the one leading the study. As I stood in front of the group of inmates, this man made a false statement concerning Jesus. Even though I really knew little about the Bible at the time, and even less about where I could find a particular Scripture, I directly refuted what the man said by using the Word of God, the Bible. This inmate made another false statement about Jesus, and again I refuted what he said by directly quoting from the Bible. I truly didn't know where these Scriptures were located, but they were hitting the target each time, and it was obvious to me that the Holy Spirit was giving me insight far beyond my own.

This exchange went on for an uncomfortably long time since I was aware that many of the other inmates were carefully analyzing everything we said. The last thing I wanted to do was make a false statement about Jesus or water down the gospel in any way. That night, by His grace, God gave me all His words needed to turn back the assault on His Son.

I learned a tremendous lesson that evening. I had recently asked God to forgive me for the time I had wasted over the years. That night I realized that the inmates could and would make statements or ask questions that would have never occurred to me. I understood that God was giving me an opportunity to make up for lost time in a hurry, and that if I was going to be effective for Him, I had better start learning His word.

This book is about real life stories of God's love, power, and triumphs—in spite of my own inadequacies—inside the walls of prison. I have changed minor details and the names of inmates to protect people and institutions from adversity.

I wish to thank many of the correctional officers whose tolerance over the years has allowed me to present the gospel of Jesus Christ under some trying circumstances. Thank you, DJ, JC, LJ, and EN, my friends and fellow volunteers, who have shown extraordinary patience toward me and my off-the-wall ways. In addition, I extend special thanks to my wife, Jenny, who spent countless hours proofing and editing my writing as I recorded these events.

INTRODUCTION

Enter through the razor wire and concrete walls of prison to experience the power of the gospel of Jesus Christ meeting head-on with the forces of evil. Be challenged and encouraged by remarkable instances of healing and deliverance from addictions, despair, rage, suicidal thoughts, the occult and more.

Read first-hand accounts of how the power of the Word of God disarms evil and brings light in the midst of suffocating darkness, hope in the midst of despair, and even prayers for victims by the prisoners themselves. Be encouraged to know that Jesus Christ is still the same yesterday, today, and forever, and that no one is beyond the power of His love to transform lives into new creations. Jesus said if anyone comes to Him, He would never turn him or her aside. You have His Word on it.

—1—

Counterfeit Armor

"That guy over there needs to talk to you," Jim whispered to me as he entered the visiting area with the rest of the inmates from maximum security. Jim, who had formerly been a high priest in the satanic church, subtly raised his tattooed arm and gestured across the room. I followed his gaze to see a muscular young man whose eyes darted around the room as he bounced lightly from one foot to the other. "He needs to talk to you in private," Jim said quietly so as not to draw attention to our conversation.

I'd known Jim for a long time, and his renunciation of Satan and embrace of Christ had always seemed genuine. His questions and insight into Scripture over the years were truly encouraging. Now he'd abruptly stopped me as I was greeting the arriving inmates. As I studied Jim carefully for a moment, he nodded and looked me straight in the eye to reassure me of his sincerity. Meanwhile the noise from the other inmates' conversations grew louder in the concrete-block visiting room.

"Are you sure, Jim?" I asked hesitantly.

Jim nodded again. "I'm glad you're here. You're the one he needs to talk to. Been praying about it and I'm sure of it." Then he quickly turned and walked away.

A moment later, another inmate came up and whispered that the new guy needed to talk to me tonight.

Ah nuts, I thought. *I hope this isn't a con.* Knowing Jim, I doubted if it was. However, I'd been teaching a lot lately, and if I'd been scheduled to teach this night, I could have passed this whole thing off to someone else. Since DJ was teaching tonight, all I needed to do was just add any insight that I could. This was supposed to be my night off. *Nuts.*

I turned and studied the newcomer for a moment. In the past, I'd found that some of these one-on-one discussions with inmates did not turn out so well. Sometimes the inmate was so deep into a cult that there was no reasoning with him. Some inmates so hardened their hearts to the Word of God that all they wanted to do was twist it or argue against it. Other times conversations would turn into a detailed recital of an inmate's past crimes, no matter how atrocious. Although I never solicited this—ever—some inmates felt the need to unload their guilt nonetheless. By the grace of God, I have never once had any nightmares or even much remembrance of these details. God has just allowed me to listen and then find scriptures that directly address whatever issues arise. The power of the Word, for men who are open to it, is life changing. The message of the cross is full assurance of God's concern for people. Little did I know that tonight I would witness one of the most incredible instances of the power of His Word I had ever experienced.

I walked over and introduced myself to the new guy, Joe. He may not have been the biggest person I'd seen in the prison, but he was plenty burly nonetheless—probably been

12

working out a lot. Something else I noticed right away about Joe was that both his hands were trembling uncontrollably. We sat down with our backs toward the rest of the group. Although only a few yards away, this was about as much privacy as the place would allow.

"Okay, Joe," I said, resigning myself to this conversation. "What's happening?"

Joe got right to the point. "Last Friday night, me and a couple of other Wiccans were doing some of our rituals together. We had a few of the Christians watching us. They would ask us questions once in a while, and I'd put them right down, no matter what they asked. They couldn't touch me with their little questions—we were doing our rituals. Not only that, but I had my armor on. They couldn't touch us; they couldn't touch me with their little questions. But then one of them asked me something that found a hole in my armor. I haven't been able to find the answer to his question. I've asked all the other witches on the tier, and no one can give me the answer. I've been up all week since then. I haven't slept, I can't eat. I've been up during the nights talking to my celly about it. He's one of those Christians. I've got to know the answer to this question. I've got to know the truth!"

I studied Joe for a minute. Whatever color his skin might once have had was drained from his face. His hollow eyes looked like two pieces of charcoal against a red blanket. And he just couldn't keep either of his hands from shaking. If he was conning me about being awake for a week straight without eating, he was doing a good job of it.

"Well, what was the question?" I wanted to know.

Joe looked at me as his eyes grew even wilder. "What will happen in the end?" Joe continued to stare at me. "I've got to know what will happen, I've got to know the truth. I've got to know!"

13

I looked into a face, into eyes that appeared totally and absolutely terrified. Joe wasn't performing any rituals or playing games tonight, and with good reason. His eternal soul was on the line, and he knew it. Then I said something to Joe that amazed me. In fact, I almost looked around behind me to see if someone else had said it. But sure enough, it came out of my mouth.

"I'm not going to give you my opinion, Joe. You don't need my opinion; you don't need any man's opinion. You need to know what God says about this."

Joe straightened up a little as he leaned slightly away from me. It was obvious to me that this was not what he expected to hear. "Okay, alright, alright," he managed to mutter. "How do we do that?"

I felt confident as I opened my Bible to Romans 3. After all, I'd been taught how to lead someone to Christ by beginning at this book using the "Roman Road." In addition, I believed in the power of God's Word to hit the mark without missing. *This should be pretty easy.* I pointed out Romans 3:23 and had Joe read the verse out loud.

"For all have sinned and fall short of the glory of God." Joe read it unfazed.

Then I turned to Romans 6:23 and had Joe read the verse aloud. "For the wages of sin is death, but the gift of God is eternal life in Christ Jesus our Lord."

Joe read the second verse sounding as cold and as dead as a stone. He began to fidget around, and I could tell his short fuse was about to ignite. It was as if I were talking to one of the concrete block walls surrounding us. No feeling, no life at all, just icy indifference.

Although I'd read in God's Word about the spiritual armor He gives His followers to wear, I didn't realize that those involved in the occult also put on spiritual armor. However,

14

instantly I knew since *that* armor was from Satan, it had to be counterfeit. I was learning on the fly here, but I knew the armor Joe had been using was phony—it had to be. And I knew there is unimaginable power in the Word of God as it is energized by the Holy Spirit. Satan's hold on this man was strong, but Jesus has almighty power. Yet at that moment, it was very clear to me by his body language that Joe was about to bolt or explode. The Word was not getting through at all. In addition, I knew God wanted Joe to know the Truth far more than I did.

Dear God, I desperately prayed as I waited for Joe to blow his top, *I know there is power in Your Word. What is wrong here?* I received an answer from God immediately. Some people may say this answer was simply my imagination, but I believe it was from the Lord. Although being admonished by God is never pleasant for me, I'd much rather hear a word of rebuke from my God than not hear from Him at all.

"Do not treat My Word as if it were some checklist, some recipe or agenda to check off one Scripture after another. My Word is alive and powerful. Now follow your heart, follow your heart, follow your heart."

My mouth suddenly felt as dry as dust as my mind raced. *Okay, Lord, but if this doesn't work real soon there's major trouble here, not the least of which is that this guy may pull my arms off and start hitting me over the head with them.*

I looked at Joe. "Okay, read this, will you?" I managed to say. "This is the meaning of life." I opened my Bible to the Book of Colossians.

Joe read aloud Colossians 1:16. "For by Him all things were created that are in heaven and that are on earth, visible and invisible, whether thrones or dominions or principalities or powers. All things were created through Him and for Him." Joe studied these Words for a few moments.

"You mean to tell me that's why we're here?" Joe asked, not trying to hide his growing aggravation. "That's why everyone is here? We're created by this Jesus and for Him? This is the meaning of life? That's why everyone is born, why everyone is created?"

I nodded. "Yes, but there's a problem," I said as I struggled to keep my opinions out of things and let God do what only He can do. I turned to Isaiah 59:2. Joe read the verse aloud. "But your iniquities have separated you from your God; And your sins have hidden His face from you, So that He will not hear."

"You mean to tell me that I was made for God, but my sins have separated me from Him so that I can't get to Him?" Joe glared at me, anger burning in his wild eyes. "Are you saying I've got to be perfect? Is that what you're saying? That I've got to be perfect?" Joe was having trouble controlling his anger and the growing volume of his voice.

Even though Joe was now getting furious, I felt the peace that surpasses understanding. By human standards, I should have been concerned for my well-being, considering whom I was sitting next to and his state of mind. Yet I knew that God's Word was breaking through, that the phony armor of Satan was starting to crumble. If I could have seen the spiritual warfare going on around us right then, I'm sure it would have been dazzling. But then I would have probably forgotten what I was supposed to be doing. I know I'm not the sharpest tool in the shed, but I had no fear at that moment, none at all.

"Well, there's one more thing you need to know," I stated as I was led to the book of 1 Peter. Joe read the words of verse 3:18: "For Christ also suffered once for sins, the just for the unjust, that He might bring us to God. . ."

Joe looked intently at this verse for a long while. Then I asked him to read it out loud again, which he did. He continued to stare at it for quite some time. Although I wanted to say something, I managed to remain silent. I've learned that when the Holy Spirit of God is working, I need to stay out of the way.

Eventually Joe looked at me and began to speak about his past, of how he'd gotten involved in witchcraft, about the meetings. As he would speak of an event in his life, I'd hold up my hand and stop him.

"Look at this," I said as God led me to a scripture that directly related to what Joe was describing. Again, Joe read it aloud.

"Wow, that's it exactly," he said. Then he began to tell me more about his life.

"Wait, look at this," I said as I turned more pages of the Word. "Read this," I prompted Joe.

Joe read the Words of life once again. "'The thief does not come except to steal, and to kill, and to destroy. I have come that they may have life, and that they may have it more abundantly'" (John 10:10). "That's it, that's exactly what happened to me!" Joe exclaimed. "I was promised so much for right now, in the present, if I followed Satan. I had a good wife, great job, big house. Now it's all been destroyed, I've lost it all."

Again and again Joe told me experiences of his life in the occult, and again and again God gave me the truth of Scriptures to challenge and answer precisely what he was saying. This went on and on until I looked up at the clock and was stunned at how much time had passed.

I realized we didn't have much left of our session together before Joe would have to go back to the tier where he lived. As I'd initially done, I now turned again to Romans

17

3:23 and 6:23. As Joe diligently read each verse aloud, this time the Words penetrated his heart. Then I turned to John 3:16 as Joe read the final scripture we were going to consider this night.

"For God so loved the world that He gave His only begotten Son, that whoever believes in Him should not perish but have everlasting life."

As he finished, I looked at him. "Okay, Joe, God has answered everything you've said about your life with His Word for well over this past hour. To the best of my ability, I've kept my opinions out of it."

Joe nodded his agreement, his eyes wide, no longer with terror, but with utter amazement.

"We've only got a short time left," I continued, "and now you know what God has to say about you and your situation. What do you want to do?"

Joe was emphatic. "I want this Jesus right now, I've got to know what will happen to me in the end, and I've got to know the truth!"

"Okay, I'll pray, and if you want to repeat after me or use your own words, that will be fine. God looks at your heart, that's what's important to Him, that's what matters, got it?"

Joe took a deep breath. "Alright, let's do it."

As I prayed, Joe made the words his own as he put everything at the foot of the cross. All the addictions, all the filth, all the wrong, all the sin. Then he stated that he believed Jesus died on the cross for him, that Christ's blood shed on the cross washed away his sins, and that Jesus was raised from the dead and is alive today. Joe asked Jesus to be his own personal Savior and thanked Him for forgiving his sins.

About this time I had a strange thought. It occurred to me that since Joe was so deep into the occult, that there would be something else, perhaps something more dramatic, to his renouncing his sins and accepting Jesus. After all, Joe was not just neutral about God; he had previously given his very soul to Satan. He was a main player in the occult at the prison. For a brief moment, I wondered why there wasn't something a little more intense. Strange how my mind works at times. But then as I prayed and Joe repeated, he asked that Jesus would now be Lord of his life from this day on. That's when it happened.

Because Joe's heart was sincere and Satan's counterfeit armor had been crushed by the Truth of the Word, the Truth of Jesus – God's power fell on Joe. The muscular young man began to tremble, but this time it was not just his hands. Now, from the top of his head to the bottom of his feet, Joe began to shake uncontrollably. We were sitting side by side on metal seats that were welded to a steel table that was bolted to a concrete floor. Had it not been so, I believe Joe would have been knocked to the ground. He then began to weep uncontrollably. Not just getting choked up or shedding a few tears, but deep, laboring sobs coming from the core of his being.

Joe tried to cover his face with his hands, but he was shaking so badly that at the same time he also needed to hang on to the heavy steel table so as not to fall off his seat. The sound of the anguished sobs and the sight of Joe's trembling shoulders and back as he labored for breath probably made my own eyes wide. I needn't have concerned myself about things being too calm.

This went on for what seemed like a long time. I am just a simple man and don't understand many things. But I know that Jesus said that when an evil spirit leaves a man it goes out to a dry place and then returns with seven more evil spirits and finds the home unoccupied, swept clean, and put in order. And the condition of that man is then worse than

19

before. So I prayed intensely for Joe that the Holy Spirit would completely and totally fill the void made by the departure of the evil one.

Finally, Joe began to gather himself together as he caught his breath.

"So tell me what's happening?" I asked quietly.

"It's gone. It's gone. The weight is all gone. It's all gone." he said softly as he looked up at the ceiling, the stain of tears visible on his face. "It's all gone. All the weight is gone!" He repeated as he continued to regain his composure, his words full of astonishment and gratitude. Then Joe turned and smiled at me.

"Now I know the truth. Now I know what will happen to me in the end. Now everything is going to be fine. Everything is going to be all right from now on."

"Well, ah, not exactly," I replied

"What do you mean?" Joe's smile quickly disappeared, replaced by a look of shock.

"Well, do you know what it's going to be like living for Jesus in a place like this? Do you have any idea how much grief you're going to catch for following Jesus in here?"

Joe looked over my shoulder at the men participating in the Bible study behind us. "Oh yeah, those guys there, most of them are Christians. And I was one to give *them* grief! I know what it's going to be like."

Then Joe looked back at me as he grew solemn. "My grandmother—she prayed for me for years and years. She never stopped praying for me. Now she's in the hospital and she's dying. I've got a forty-year sentence, and I'll never get to see her again. She never stopped praying for me. She never stopped."

Not too terribly often, but occasionally I get a good idea. "Well, you can write her, can't you?"

Joe's face lit up as he nodded.

"Then write her about all that has happened tonight and this past week. Write it all down, and mail it to her soon. Don't wait, do it soon."

Joe agreed and then the loud electronic lock on the heavy steel exit door sounded and interrupted us, effectively ending the session.

After all the inmates left the room, my friend DJ, who was teaching the lesson that night, came over and asked me how it went. When I told him what had taken place, he then told me about a remarkable thing which occurred as he was teaching.

"I don't think I've ever had this happen to me before," DJ stated. "Right in the middle of my lesson, one of the prisoners interrupted me and asked me to stop. Then he asked everyone to pray for what was going on with you and Joe, that Joe would give up the Satan worship and accept Christ before our time was over tonight. Joe must have been driving those guys crazy all week."

"Thanks for stopping to do that." I said sincerely.

DJ looked at me. "From what you told me, I'm glad we did. Sounds to me like a war was going on."

Before coming to the Bible study that night, Joe had gone a week with little or no sleep or food as he was being confronted with the Truth. Jesus told us that it is the work of the Holy Spirit to convict people of sin, righteousness, and judgment. Apparently, the Holy Spirit would not let Joe alone. Joe could have accepted Jesus as his Lord and Savior anytime during that week, yet he didn't. It wasn't until after I myself had learned some valuable lessons about the Word that I was privileged to lead him to the Lord. I think now of those inmates' prayers for this man and the prayers of a grandmother who would not give up on her prison-bound grandson no matter how grim things looked. I simply got to be in on the harvest where others had labored.

While I was listening to Joe during those very intense minutes when we were sitting side by side, I know there were scriptures God gave me that I had not read in a year or more. When I looked up at the clock during our discussion, I was shocked to see that one hour and twenty minutes had passed since we had started the session! Eighty minutes of discussing one scripture after another, each one hitting the mark dead-on. If I was relying on my own ability, I could not have come up with scriptures to last eighty seconds. Not sitting next to a very desperate man in maximum security, the most violent part of the prison. A man who had a heart as hard as a rock, given totally to Satan, and who looked like he was about to go crazy. Indeed, not anywhere, at any time. Since this experience, I try not to answer questions with my own opinion. I instead rely on the Words of the One Who knows the answers to all our questions. To God be all the glory.

> For the word of God is living and powerful, and sharper than any two-edged sword, piercing even to the division of soul and spirit, and of joints and marrow, and is a discerner of the thoughts and intents of the heart (Hebrews 4:12).

> All Scripture is God-breathed and is useful for teaching, rebuking, correcting and training in righteousness so that the man of God may be thoroughly equipped for every good work (2 Timothy 3:16-17 NIV).

> I will give them an undivided heart and put a new spirit in them; I will remove from them their heart of stone and give them a heart of flesh. Then they will follow my decrees and be careful to keep my laws. They will be my people, and I will be their God (Ezekiel 11:19-20 NIV).

"Is not My word like a fire," says the LORD, "and like a hammer that breaks the rock in pieces?" (Jeremiah 23:29).

Then the LORD said to Moses, "Is there any limit to my power? Now you will see whether or not my word comes true!" (Numbers 11:23 NLT).

For with God nothing is ever impossible and no word from God shall be without power or impossible of fulfillment (Luke 1:37 AMP).

For by Him all things were created that are in heaven and that are on earth, visible and invisible, whether thrones or dominions or principalities or powers. All things were created through Him and for Him (Colossians 1:16).

Say to them, "As surely as I live," declares the Sovereign LORD, "I take no pleasure in the death of the wicked, but rather that they turn from their ways and live. Turn! Turn from your evil ways . . ." (Ezekiel 33:11 NIV).

The weapons we fight with are not the weapons of the world. On the contrary, they have divine power to demolish strongholds. We demolish arguments and every pretension that sets itself up against the knowledge of God, and we take captive every thought to make it obedient to Christ (2 Corinthians 10:4-5 NIV).

The thief comes only to steal and kill and destroy; I have come that they may have life, and have it to the full (John 10:10 NIV).

Finally, my brethren, be strong in the Lord and in the power of His might. Put on the whole armor of God, that you may be able to stand against the wiles of the devil. For we do not wrestle against flesh and blood, but against principalities, against powers, against the rulers of the darkness of this age, against spiritual hosts of wickedness in the heavenly places. Therefore take up the whole armor of God, that you may be able to withstand in the evil day, and having done all, to stand. Stand therefore, having girded your waist with truth, having put on the breastplate of righteousness, and having shod your feet with the preparation of the gospel of peace; above all, taking the shield of faith with which you will be able to quench all the fiery darts of the wicked one. And take the helmet of salvation, and the sword of the Spirit, which is the word of God . . . (Ephesians 6:10-17).

That if you confess with your mouth, "Jesus is Lord," and believe in your heart that God raised him from the dead, you will be saved. For it is with your heart that you believe and are justified, and it is with your mouth that you confess and are saved (Romans 10:9-10 NIV).

Yes, and all who desire to live godly in Christ Jesus will suffer persecution (2 Timothy 3:12).

And I will pray the Father, and He will give you another Helper, that He may abide with you forever—the Spirit of truth, whom the world cannot receive, because it neither sees Him nor knows Him; but you know Him, for He dwells with you and will be in you. I will not leave you orphans; I will come to you (John 14:16-18).

However, when He, the Spirit of truth, has come, He will guide you into all truth; for He will not speak on His own authority, but whatever He hears He will speak; and He will tell you things to come (John 16:13).

But we belong to God; that is why those who know God listen to us. If they do not belong to God, they do not listen to us. That is how we know if someone has the Spirit of truth or the spirit of deception (1 John 4:6 NLT).

For this is good and acceptable in the sight of God our Savior, who desires all men to be saved and to come to the knowledge of the truth (1 Timothy 2:3-4)

But we are bound to give thanks to God always for you, brethren beloved by the Lord, because God from the beginning chose you for salvation through sanctification by the Spirit and belief in the truth . . . (2 Thessalonians 2:13).

Pilate therefore said to Him, "Are You a king then?" Jesus answered, "You say rightly that I am a king. For this cause I was born, and for this cause I have come into the world, that I should bear witness to the truth. Everyone who is of the truth hears My voice" (John 18:37).

— 2 —

Twenty-One Years

Once in a great while, a prisoner who appears to want nothing to do with us Christian volunteers will attend our Bible studies. Such was the case with Ivan. Because the glass in the door through which the inmates enter our visiting room is made of one-way mirror, we volunteers can't see who is behind the door until it is opened. When Ivan would come in, he would brush right past me, even if I had my right hand outstretched to greet him. After all, Ivan had an image to uphold, and he would not allow anyone to see him with his guard down for even an instant.

After the event that I'm about to describe took place, I learned some things about Ivan. Apparently, when he was out in the recreation yard one day, he bumped into an inmate who was quite a bit bigger than he was. Jail-code demands that the subordinate inmate apologize and step out of the way. But Ivan, as small as he was, didn't wish to step aside. The larger inmate told Ivan that he would kill him right then and there. Ivan produced a shim (a homemade prison knife) and told the larger man to "come on, kill me right now, come on." I don't know what happened after that, but if I, as a volunteer, heard about this event that had taken place years before, no doubt all the prisoners had heard as well. I also learned that when Ivan came up a crowded stairway, inmates would move to either side to get out of his way. For me, knowing about these incidents just highlights the glory of Almighty God, Who alone is able to break the hardest of hearts with the Truth of His Son Jesus.

My friend DJ, who had been volunteering at the prison for several years, came up to me at the beginning of a session.

"That guy over there, Ivan, he wants to say something to the group," DJ said quietly to me.

DJ knew as well as I that we never know what to expect when a prisoner wants to say something to the group. It could be filled with colorful language; it could have some theology taken out of context, or mixed in with some really weird beliefs he'd picked up somewhere in his life; it might be a statement berating the prison or a correctional officer. So it is always with reservation that we allow an inmate to address the group, especially someone about whom none of us knew the first thing. I don't think Ivan had even said as much as hello in all the times he'd attended our studies.

"Well, okay," I nodded tentatively to DJ. "Thanks for warning me. If he wants to say something, let's hope we can do damage control when he's done."

DJ gave Ivan the okay and the diminutive man stood up next to his empty table. Ivan always sat alone and tonight was no exception.

"I heard somewhere the Bible says you're supposed to give account of yourself, so I'm gonna do that," he began.

I felt things in me begin to pucker up.

"I've been in prison for twenty-one years. I've seen a lot of things in twenty-one years. Lots of things."

I thought to myself, *I'll bet you have. But where is this going? Surely you're not going to recap twenty-one years of prison life.*

Ivan continued. "I don't figure there's much I haven't seen in my twenty-one years in this place. And I'll tell you right now, I've learned to hate. That's what gets me through the day, that's what keeps me going. That's all I know. And I've been thinking about the people who put me in this place. I've had a long time to think about them. When I get out, I've been planning on how I'm going to hurt everyone who ever hurt me. I've got a good plan, too. Ain't no one going to catch me this time. I'm going to hurt everyone who had something to do with putting me in here, and they're not going to catch me, they're not going to put me back in here. I've had twenty-one years to plan it. It's a good plan. I've gone over it a lot in my mind."

By this time Ivan had everyone's rapt attention.

"And I've been coming up here for a while now," he continued. "Listening to you people talk about this *Jesus* when I come up here. This *Jesus* this and this *Jesus* that. I've been coming up here for a while and listening to you. So the other day when I was alone, I knelt down by my bed, and I called out to this Jesus. I reached up my hand to this Jesus, just like this."

Ivan reached his right hand up over his head to show just what he'd done. Then he looked at us Christian volunteers as he put his hand down.

"Now I don't know if I said the words just right. I don't know if I said them exactly the way you people up here say them. But now – now I don't hate anymore. I don't hate anyone anymore. After twenty-one years of hating everyone, I don't hate anymore. Hate's what got me through each day. Now I don't hate, and it's all I can remember ever doing. Now I don't know what to do. Will somebody here please tell me

29

what to do, because now I don't know what to do."

Then Ivan abruptly sat down.

The room was dead silent as I cut my eyes around to the other three volunteers, no one knowing what to do or say. After a long period of silence, I finally felt prompted to speak.

"First of all, Ivan," I began slowly, "don't ever let anyone tell you that you didn't say the words just right or the exact way that they would've said them. God looks at your heart. Your heart is what matters to God. And the fact that you no longer hate is evidence that your heart was right before God when you called out to Him, and you said the words just exactly right. Don't ever doubt that, or doubt that God heard you."

Ivan stared at me and nodded slowly.

I waited a moment, hoping someone else would have some words of wisdom, but no one said anything.

"Well, Ivan, the next thing you should do," I continued, "is get yourself a Bible if you don't already have one, and start reading. I suggest you read the Gospel of John first. If you want to discuss that, or anything else from the Bible, just come back and we'll talk about it."

Ivan did get himself a Bible and began reading it, but before long, he was transferred to another institution. Like so many who either get released, moved to another living unit in the prison, or get transferred out of the area, we never knew what happened to him. I'm just eternally grateful to the God Who hears when someone sincerely cries out to Him. He hears even when the person calling to Him has been steeped in hatred for decades. And God, Almighty God, can remove every trace of that hatred in an instant. Only God!

"But He said, "The things which are impossible with men are possible with God" (Luke 18:27).

"What do you mean, 'If I can'?" Jesus asked. "Anything is possible if a person believes" (Mark 9:23 NLT).

But the Lord said to Samuel, "Do not look at his appearance or at his physical stature, because I have refused him. For the Lord does not see as man sees; for man looks at the outward appearance, but the Lord looks at the heart" (1 Samuel 16:7)

So God, who knows the heart, acknowledged them by giving them the Holy Spirit, just as He did to us, and made no distinction between us and them, purifying their hearts by faith (Acts 15:8-9).

And I will give you a new heart with new and right desires, and I will put a new spirit in you. I will take out your stony heart of sin and give you a new, obedient heart (Ezekiel 36:26 NLT).

This is what the Lord says: "Cursed are those who put their trust in mere humans and turn their hearts away from the Lord. They are like stunted shrubs in the desert, with no hope for the future. They will live in the barren wilderness, on the salty flats where no one lives.
"But blessed are those who trust in the Lord and have made the Lord their hope and confidence. They are like trees planted along a riverbank, with roots that reach deep into the water. Such trees are not bothered by the heat or worried by long months of drought. Their leaves stay green, and they go right on producing delicious fruit.
"The human heart is most deceitful and desperately wicked. Who really knows how bad it is? But I know! I,

31

the LORD, search all hearts and examine secret motives. I give all people their due rewards, according to what their actions deserve" (Jeremiah 17:5-10 NLT).

Seek the LORD while He may be found, Call upon Him while He is near. Let the wicked forsake his way, And the unrighteous man his thoughts; Let him return to the LORD, And He will have mercy on him; And to our God, For He will abundantly pardon. "For My thoughts are not your thoughts, Nor are your ways My ways," says the LORD. "For as the heavens are higher than the earth, So are My ways higher than your ways, And My thoughts than your thoughts. For as the rain comes down, and the snow from heaven, And do not return there, But water the earth, And make it bring forth and bud, That it may give seed to the sower And bread to the eater, So shall My word be that goes forth from My mouth; It shall not return to Me void, But it shall accomplish what I please, And it shall prosper in the thing for which I sent it" (Isaiah 55:6-11).

Nor is there salvation in any other, for there is no other name under heaven given among men by which we must be saved (Acts 4:12).

For I am not ashamed of the gospel of Christ, for it is the power of God to salvation for everyone who believes, for the Jew first and also for the Greek. For in it the righteousness of God is revealed from faith to faith; as it is written, "The just shall live by faith" (Romans 1:16-17).

And He ordered us to preach to the people, and solemnly to testify that this is the One who has been appointed by God as Judge of the living and the dead. Of Him all the prophets bear witness that through His name everyone who believes in Him receives forgiveness of sins (Acts 10:42-43 NASB).

For the message of the cross is foolishness to those who are perishing, but to us who are being saved it is the power of God (1 Corinthians 1:18).

And it shall come to pass That whoever calls on the name of the LORD Shall be saved (Acts 2:21).

—3—

The Letter

Over the years, I've seen a few men who are very despondent show up at our prison Bible studies. Although not trying to disrespect us, they tend to sit off by themselves. They generally have a blank look in their eyes when we greet them coming or going. Usually they don't return for more than a few studies. But on the rare occasion when they keep attending—and remain in a depressed state—I begin to wonder how close they may be to ending things once and for all. Myron was one of these men. The best thing I know to do at such a time is what we always do: pray and continue to present the gospel of Jesus Christ as clearly and as scripturally as we can.

One day Myron came into the service lit up as if he'd just been given a "Get out of Jail Free" card. He was jumping around and struggling to get the words out as he came up to me while the rest of the group milled about finding seats. I had never heard Myron speak so many words in all the time I'd known him.

"God is real, man, He is really real, did you know that?" Myron exclaimed to me as he tried to contain himself. "God's real!"

"Well, yeah, I know that," I said, wondering if he thought we volunteers come up to the prison because we don't have anyone else to hang out with on the outside. "I know He's real, Myron, or I wouldn't be here right now. What's happened to you?"

"Oh man, let me tell you," he replied. "Last week when I left here, I was at the end of it. I'd had enough and I was at the end. I lay down on my bed, the bottom bunk, and I just stared at the bottom of my celly's bunk above me. I just stared at it and started praying. I guess that's what you'd call it. I just said real quiet like, 'God, I don't know if you're real or not or if the Bible is real or not. I hear those volunteers up here talk about You like You're really alive, like You care. I don't know if anything the guys up at the Bible study say is true or not or if it's just a bunch of junk. I don't know if You're real or not, God.'"

Myron stared at me with wide eyes. I just nodded, wanting to hear what happened before anyone started eavesdropping on our conversation.

"So I said something like this," Myron continued. "'God, there is no one who even knows I'm alive, no one who even cares if I'm alive or dead. The last person to care about me was my father, and I haven't heard from him in eleven years, God. He doesn't even know where I am or if I'm still alive. I don't even know if *he's* still alive. No one knows or cares about me, whether I'm dead or alive, God, no one.'

"'But God, those guys up at the Bible study act like they know You're real. So I'm asking You, God, to show me. Let me know that You're alive, please. Just something, anything. Let me know that You are real, that You are alive, that You care. That You really are real, God. Please, God, I'm at the end of it here, please.'"

Myron looked at me as he paused a moment. "After I prayed, I just kept staring at the bottom of the bunk over me, waiting. I was trying to listen for anything, maybe see something, maybe feel something. I don't know what I was doing. I just wanted to be open to God letting me know that He was real, somehow, someway.

"After a long time I started to get sleepy, but I fought it. I was at the end, and I didn't want to fall asleep so as to miss God if He did something. I tried to stay awake as long as I could, but finally I got so sleepy I started to doze off. Then I thought – if He's God, then He can let me see Him in my dreams or else wake me up. So I let myself go to sleep.

"When I woke up in the morning I looked around. Nothing. I lay there for a while, hoping, for something, anything. But nothing happened. I was at the end of it. I got up as quietly as I could and saw my celly's mail that had been slid through the door slot and was lying on the floor. I put it on the corner of his bed, and then I opened the door as quietly as I could and slipped outside, trying not to wake up my celly. I looked all around the day-room, but nothing looked different. Everything looked the same, just the same old way it always looked. Nothing was different, nothing.

"Still, I guess I was hoping against hope that God would show me something, but my hope was about gone. I walked around the day-room, trying to see or hear or sense something from God, but there was nothing. Same guys playing cards, same guard. Nothing different from any other time.

"I sat down and looked at the floor. *Well, I did the best I could*, I thought to myself. *I gave this God a chance. If there even is a God, I reckon He don't care nothing about me.*

37

"Just then my celly came out of our room and walked over to me," Myron said, his eyes dancing. "He tossed a letter at me."

"'Why did you put this on my bed?'" my celly wanted to know.

"I never get any mail," Myron confided in me, "so I never even bothered to look at the names and addresses on the mail that morning."

Then Myron got all choked up, a definite no-no in the prison. For if a prisoner shows any sentiment or emotion, especially tears, then the predators will see it and take advantage of it to the utmost. Although Myron knew this far better than I did, he was now having serious trouble controlling his emotions.

"You see," he managed to get out, "it was a letter from my dad. Eleven years and I'd not heard from him. Not a word. And then this day, of all days when..." Myron closed his eyes as he gathered himself together. "God is real, man," he whispered. "He's real."

Myron looked down and made his way to his seat, trying to hide his red face and eyes.

I looked away as quickly as I could, not wanting to point out his emotion to any of the others in the room. Myron had told me all he could that night. Indeed, all he needed to.

When I think of God's timing in Myron's situation, I am in awe of the God Who loves us. Myron's father sat down from who knows where to write a letter to a son whom he'd not heard from in eleven years. And he mailed it on just a certain day. I'm sure there are many different ways a letter can be delayed or speeded up or rerouted or lost somewhere, both outside and inside the prison system. Eleven years, that is over four thousand days. A day earlier and it might not have meant as much to Myron. A day later might well have been too late for that man's eternal soul. Eleven years. The odds of that letter arriving just when it did have to be close to impossible. Impossible, at least for man. God is so real!

Surely the arm of the Lord is not too short to save, nor his ear too dull to hear (Isaiah 59:1 NIV).

"Am I only a God nearby," declares the LORD, "and not a God far away? Can anyone hide in secret places so that I cannot see him?" declares the LORD. "Do not I fill heaven and earth?" declares the LORD (Jeremiah 23:23-24 NIV).

'Behold, I am the LORD, the God of all flesh; is anything too difficult for Me?' (Jeremiah 32:27 NASB).

In his hand is the life of every creature and the breath of all mankind (Job 12:10 NIV).

O LORD, you have searched me and you know me. You know when I sit and when I rise; you perceive my thoughts from afar. You discern my going out and my lying down; you are familiar with all my ways. Before a word is on my tongue you know it completely, O LORD. You hem me in—behind and before; you have laid your hand upon me. Such knowledge is too wonderful for me, too lofty for me to attain. Where can I go from your Spirit? Where can I flee from your presence? If I go up to the heavens, you are there; if I make my bed in the depths, you are there. If I rise on the wings of the dawn, if I settle on the far side of the sea, even there your hand will guide me, your right hand will hold me fast. If I say, "Surely the darkness will hide me and the light become night around me," even the darkness will not be dark to you; the night will shine like the day, for darkness is as light to you. For you created my inmost being; you knit me together in my mother's womb. I praise you because I am fearfully and wonderfully made; your works are wonderful, I know that full well. My frame was not hidden from you when I was made in the secret place. When I was woven together in the depths of the earth, your eyes saw my unformed body. All the days ordained for me were written in your book before one of them came to be. How precious to me are your thoughts, O God! How vast is the sum of them! Were I to count them, they would outnumber the grains of sand. When I awake, I am still with you (Psalm 139:1-18 NIV).

The Spirit of the Sovereign Lord is on me, because the Lord has anointed me to preach good news to the poor. He has sent me to bind up the brokenhearted, to proclaim freedom for the captives and release from darkness for the prisoners (Isaiah 61:1 NLT).

So humble yourselves under the mighty power of God, and in his good time he will honor you. Give all your worries and cares to God, for he cares about what happens to you (1 Peter 5:6-7 NLT).

But Jesus looked at them and said, "With men it is impossible, but not with God; for with God all things are possible" (Mark 10:27).

The God who made the world and everything in it is the Lord of heaven and earth and does not live in temples built by hands. And he is not served by human hands, as if he needed anything, because he himself gives all men life and breath and everything else. From one man he made every nation of men, that they should inhabit the whole earth; and he determined the times set for them and the exact places where they should live. God did this so that men would seek him and perhaps reach out for him and find him, though he is not far from each one of us (Acts 17:24-27 NIV).

—4—

Inside Out

A one-way mirror is at the entrance to one of our meeting rooms at the prison. Because of this, it is difficult for us to see who is on the other side of the door and who will be first into the room. There is a murky haze that covers the glass, not unlike the spiritual darkness that I've sometimes felt enveloping the prison. For certain prisoners, this darkened glass can be a real advantage as they can see us but we can't see them until they come through the door.

On this particular night, the other three volunteers were several feet away and I was the one nearest the entrance. Had I seen who was ready to launch himself into the room and run up to me screaming, it would have made no difference. I had never seen this man before, so I had no way to know to prepare myself, if indeed that was even possible. As the electronic lock sounded and the heavy steel door swung open, a young man named Mike raced into the room and planted himself a few inches from my face, yelling incoherently.

Mike then glared at me, apparently to gauge my reaction. For whatever reason, I've found that I often come up with just the perfect response to what people say or do—about two hours later. As it was, this time I just stared back at the man towering three or four inches over me, his muscular arms covered with tattoos. When Mike realized that was all the reaction he was going to get out of me, he sneered menacingly, strutted off, and plopped himself down in a chair.

We greeted the other men as they came in and then began our Bible study. Or at least we tried to. It seems Mike didn't care much about any Bible study. He was more interested in being the center of attention. His snide remarks were numerous and crude. We finally got through the study and the inmates left the room.

"Man, you ever seen that guy before?" another volunteer asked.

We all shook our heads. "I hope he doesn't ever come back," someone added.

"You got that right," agreed another.

From past experience, I think all of us realized that Mike had no interest in the Bible, and figured he probably wouldn't be back often, if at all.

We were wrong.

During much of the next several months, my friend, DJ, and I seemed to be the only ones consistently available for our weekly Bible studies at the prison. And I don't believe Mike ever missed a single one of them.

DJ and I took turns teaching, and when it was my turn, I remember praying, "Lord, please let Mike forget what night this is, or let him get moved to another unit, or let him not want to come to the studies anymore. We're trying to teach Your Word, here, God, and there are men showing up who are trying to learn. You know that, God. But Mike keeps interrupting and trying to destroy the study and mock what You're doing here, Lord. Please don't let him show up tonight. Don't let him come back, ever."

Sure enough, the next week Mike would be there, right on time. He was extremely sharp-witted, and could come up with a cutting comment or question at a moment's notice and sidetrack an entire study in just seconds. Then he'd follow it up with another obnoxious comment and go off on a tangent, and we'd get flustered as we tried to regroup and get back on track. Mike was an expert at derailing us, and no matter what we tried, there seemed to be no way we could stop him.

I remember being at my wit's end coming down the stairs to the lobby after trying to teach one night. "You know, I wish Mike would never come back. I just seem to get started and then he makes some cutting remark and then another guy will join in and it turns into a mess. That guy is so quick, and I get so frustrated. Once in a while something he says is downright hilarious, but I don't dare laugh, lest he think it's a green light for him to take over the whole session. But most of it's so crude and disruptive, we don't need it up here during a Bible study," I whined.

DJ looked at me and smiled. "Well, you know we did pray before the session that God would bring up the men He wanted to and keep away the men He wanted to. We did pray that, you know?"

I'd grumble about maybe remembering praying something like that. I was just glad that I didn't have to teach for a couple of weeks.

The next week as we came down the steps after the session, it was DJ who had tried to lead the study.

"You know," DJ huffed, "I've got half a mind to ask the guards to never let that guy back into one of these Bible studies again. He is obnoxious, and he just tries to take over and be the center of attention. There's no way someone can teach when he's in there. He's just obnoxious."

I smiled and looked at DJ. "Well, you know, we did pray before the session..."

This went on for quite some time. Both of us were praying that God, in His perfect timing, would remove Mike. We were trying our best to trust Him, but the situation was getting just about intolerable. We knew we were still speaking His Word inside the prison, albeit with much difficulty. But DJ and I continued to help each other as best we could. Now that I know the outcome, I think it was what the Bible refers to as "iron sharpening iron."

Finally, after months of Mike's obnoxious behavior, something strange began to happen.

"Have you noticed something weird about Mike?" I asked DJ one night after a Bible study.

"Yeah, I have. Lately he just comes in and sits and listens. Then he gets up and leaves after the study. No more cutting or obnoxious remarks. Only a few comments now and then, and even those are pretty mild."

I nodded my agreement. "Did you notice I got through the entire study tonight and Mike didn't even say a word?"

"I noticed that," DJ replied. "I wonder if he's sick or something."

One night Mike entered the room for one of the sessions, and he was a sight to behold. He had a big black eye and was cut up pretty badly. No one said a word about it as we took our seats. Although Mike was young and big and muscular, it seems there's always someone bigger and stronger somewhere in the prison system.

Well what do you know? I thought smugly, *Mike finally popped off to someone bigger than himself and that someone didn't much like it.* After all the grief he'd given us week after week and month after month, I remember feeling glad that he was apparently on the losing side of a fight.

But Mike kept coming to the Bible studies. He was quiet for several more weeks, and then he began to speak out again. Only this time it was different. He still kept his extremely quick and dry wit about him, but now his comments seemed to be more in line with the study, and they'd lost their critical edge. Some of his comments were actually round-about questions that seemed to warrant honest answers about the Bible. And some of his off-center comments were so funny it was no longer possible to keep from laughing along with the rest of the group. This went on for several more weeks. Then one night Mike spoke words that humbled me to my core and still humble me to this day.

"I talked to my dad the other day," Mike began quietly. "You guys probably know that when we call out of here we have to call collect. Anyway, me and my dad, we don't get along too well."

I smiled to myself. *I can understand that.*

"So," Mike continued, "when he picked up the phone and I heard the operator tell him who was calling, I just started talking. 'Don't hang up on me, Dad, don't hang up on me. I've got something really important I've got to tell you, Dad. So don't hang up on me, Dad, please don't hang up.'

"Well, he didn't hang up and I got to talk to him. I told him about Jesus and about what He means to me and how He's changed me. How I'm not who I used to be. I told my dad all about Him, or at least all that I know about Him. My dad listened the whole time, which is pretty amazing in itself. He didn't interrupt. He didn't say much, and he didn't hang up on me. I guess he must have figured out I was telling him the truth, 'cause I was. Finally, for once in my life, I was telling him the truth, and he picked up on that. He can figure me out pretty good, always has been able to. When I finally got done talking there was this sort of silence for a while. Then he told me that if this Jesus could make this kind of change in me, then he wanted to know Him too. So, on a collect call from inside here to the outside, I led my dad to the Lord."

We stared at Mike, stunned.

"So, you asked Jesus to be your Lord and Savior?"

Mike nodded. "Yeah, a little while ago."

"Man, why didn't you say something sooner?"

Mike looked at us and just shook his head, and I could see the pain in his eyes. I didn't pursue it any further right then, but later in one-on-one conversations with him, I think I finally figured it out. Although he never said it in so many words, it seemed Mike had trusted people before in his young life, and gotten burned and deeply hurt. He wanted to make sure this Jesus was real before he came out and said anything to us or anyone else. I am so grateful he took that chance on Jesus and found out how real He is.

A short time later DJ and I learned that the reason Mike had come in so beat up one night was because another inmate had picked a fight with him. Afterward one of the correctional officers came up to Mike and asked him, "Man, what's the matter with you? You could have torn that guy apart, but you didn't even fight back. What's with you, man?"

Apparently, Mike looked the officer in the eye and said, "I've accepted Jesus Christ as my Lord and Savior, and I will fight no more."

As soon as I heard that, the Lord immediately put His Word on my heart: "In your struggle against sin, you have not yet resisted to the point of shedding your blood." (Hebrews 12:4 NIV). Mike took that beating because he gave himself to Jesus. I never have taken a beating for believing in my Lord Jesus, and I don't know what I would have done if I had been in Mike's position. And I remembered immediately how I had been so smug and so glad that someone had beaten Mike up. When I realized that Mike had taken that pounding because he wouldn't deny Jesus, I was cut to the heart. I had to ask God to forgive me once again for my arrogance. Jesus has a lot to say to us about judging others. A lot.

I also remembered how I'd prayed for God to take Mike out of our Bible studies, especially when it was my turn to teach. And I remember wondering why God wouldn't do it, or how could it be that He couldn't see how disruptive Mike was and how it was hurting our Bible studies. Yet once again, God had it all under control.

Jesus never said He died on that cross to make us comfortable in our little plans in life. He died so we could get our sins forgiven and get right with Him. His horrific agony on that cross was anything but comfortable for Him. Had He answered my prayers to keep me in my comfort zone, two souls, both in the prison of this world's darkness, one inside an institution and one outside, might never have known Jesus the Christ, the True Light of Life.

There was a man sent from God, whose name was John. This man came for a witness, to bear witness of the Light, that all through him might believe. He was not that Light, but was sent to bear witness of that Light. That was the true Light which gives light to every man coming into the world. He was in the world, and the world was made through Him, and the world did not know Him. He came to His own, and His own did not receive Him. But as many as received Him, to them He gave the right to become children of God, to those who believe in His name: who were born, not of blood, nor of the will of the flesh, nor of the will of man, but of God (John 1:6-13).

But Jesus answered them, saying, "The hour has come that the Son of Man should be glorified. Most assuredly, I say to you, unless a grain of wheat falls into the ground and dies, it remains alone; but if it dies, it produces much grain. He who loves his life will lose it, and he who hates his life in this world will keep it for eternal life. If anyone serves Me, let him follow Me; and where I am, there My servant will be also. If anyone serves Me, him My Father will honor.

"Now My soul is troubled, and what shall I say? 'Father, save Me from this hour?' But for this purpose I came to this hour. Father, glorify Your name." Then a voice came from heaven, saying, "I have both glorified it and will glorify it again." Therefore the people who stood by and heard it said that it had thundered. Others said, "An angel has spoken to Him." Jesus answered and said, "This voice did not come because of Me, but for your sake. Now is the judgment of this world; now the ruler of this world will be cast out. And I, if I am lifted up from the earth, will draw all peoples to Myself." This He said, signifying by what death He would die (John 12:23-33).

Then He said to them, "These are the words which I spoke to you while I was still with you, that all things must be fulfilled which were written in the Law of Moses and the Prophets and the Psalms concerning Me." And He opened their understanding, that they might comprehend the Scriptures. Then He said to them, "Thus it is written, and thus it was necessary for the Christ to suffer and to rise from the dead the third day, and that repentance and remission of sins should be preached in His name to all nations, beginning at Jerusalem" (Luke 24:44-47).

For the Son of Man has come to seek and to save that which was lost (Luke 19:10).

Therefore, since we are surrounded by such a great cloud of witnesses, let us throw off everything that hinders and the sin that so easily entangles, and let us run with perseverance the race marked out for us. Let us fix our eyes on Jesus, the author and perfecter of our faith, who for the joy set before him endured the cross, scorning its shame, and sat down at the right hand of the throne of God. Consider him who endured such opposition from sinful men, so that you will not grow weary and lose heart. In your struggle against sin, you have not yet resisted to the point of shedding your blood (Hebrews 12:1-4 NIV).

For what credit is it if, when you are beaten for your faults, you take it patiently? But when you do good and suffer, if you take it patiently, this is commendable before God (1 Peter 2:20).

Do not judge, or you too will be judged. For in the same way you judge others, you will be judged, and with the measure you use, it will be measured to you. Why do you look at the speck of sawdust in your brother's eye and pay no attention to the plank in your own eye? How can you say to your brother, 'Let me take the speck out of your eye,' when all the time there is a plank in your own eye? You hypocrite, first take the plank out of your own eye, and then you will see clearly to remove the speck from your brother's eye (Matthew 7:1-5 NIV).

Let us not become weary in doing good, for at the proper time we will reap a harvest if we do not give up (Galatians 6:9 NIV).

[T]hat He would grant you, according to the riches of His glory, to be strengthened with might through His Spirit in the inner man, that Christ may dwell in your hearts through faith; that you, being rooted and grounded in love, may be able to comprehend with all the saints what is the width and length and depth and height— to know the love of Christ which passes knowledge; that you may be filled with all the fullness of God. Now to Him who is able to do exceedingly abundantly above all that we ask or think, according to the power that works in us, to Him be glory in the church by Christ Jesus to all generations, forever and ever. Amen (Ephesians 3:16-21).

—5—

The Blood of the Lamb

It is unusual for us to finish our study before time is up and the inmates have to go back to their cells, or "houses", as they call them. However, on this particular night, a rare occurrence took place and we finished more than ten minutes early. As DJ and I stood visiting with the prisoners, an inmate named Phil came over and asked if he could have a few minutes in private with the two of us.

We moved away from the others and sat down, Phil sitting between DJ and me at a small, square table. Knowing time was short, he got right to the point.

"I've been hearing voices. Two of them. They keep telling me to do bad things. Evil things. To the guys around me. I've been trying to deal with them, but they're harassing me, they won't leave me alone. And they're wearing me down; I don't know how much longer I can put up with them. I don't want to do nothing bad; I don't want to hurt nobody anymore. I need help."

As Phil looked at me, his eyes were cold, almost glazed over. There was little life in them that I could see. He looked like someone who had been in a long battle and was about to give up, if he hadn't already. I'm sure my own eyes grew wide at his words as DJ spoke up.

"Has there ever been a time when you've accepted Jesus Christ into your life?"

Phil nodded as he slowly turned his huge head towards my friend. "Yeah, a while ago. But I've done so much bad in my life. I mean some really bad things. I just figured that this sort of thing is something I deserve for all the bad I've done."

From my study of Scripture, I don't believe anyone who has accepted Christ can be possessed by a demon, but hadn't the apostle Paul been harassed by the likes of these vile things? Possessed by a demon, no, but oppressed? Once again I was learning on the fly, and once again there wasn't a lot of time to sort all this out in deep theological discussion.

"You see," Phil was saying, "I've really done a lot of evil in my life, in my younger days." He went on to enlighten us about some of those things, and I suppose, to justify in his own mind why he deserved to suffer wicked voices harassing him day and night. He spoke of a board game that had opened the door to the occult in his life, and then he told us about some of his worst crimes. On and on Phil talked as he sat to my left, DJ sitting across from me at our little metal table. I glanced at the clock. In a few minutes Phil was going to leave this room and head back to a bit of hell on earth, where all manner of evil presides and flourishes. If he didn't get relief now, he might never get it. And a lot of folks might get hurt as a result.

As Phil continued spilling out his wretched story, I sent an unspoken, critically urgent prayer to my God for help. *God, I have nothing of my own to offer this man, no human philosophy, no worldly advice, no wisdom from a university. He needs Your power and he needs it right now. Please help us.*

The answer was instantaneous, arriving—I think—before I even finished my prayer. I looked at Phil as he continued spewing out his abominable past. At last he took a breath and I interrupted.

"Have you ever read the Gospels?" I asked quickly.

Phil looked a little surprised as he slowly nodded, his eyes still glazed and faraway. "Yes, I've read them."

"Have you ever read about the crucifixion?" I asked urgently, knowing full well that the officers might open the door at any moment and our session would end.

Phil nodded.

"Did you read where they drove the nails into the hands and feet of Jesus when the soldier nailed Him to that cross?" I asked as I looked first at Phil, then at the palms of my hands as I rested them on the cold table.

Phil looked at my hands, and then he looked at the palm of his own huge right hand. Then he muttered softly. "Yes, I've read about that."

"Do you think that when the soldier drove the nails through the hands of Jesus," I held an imaginary spike in my left hand as I held it to the palm of my right, "that some of the blood of Jesus got on the hands of that soldier?"

"Yeah, I reckon it did," Phil said hesitantly as he continued to study his own hand and imagine what that must have been like.

"And, do you remember what Jesus said as he hung from the cross and looked down at that soldier who had His very blood on his hands?"

Phil looked up and studied me for a long moment. Then he tilted his head a little to the side and almost whispered the words, as if they might shatter if said too roughly, precious as they are.

"'Father, forgive them?'" Phil asked, barely audibly.

At that moment I saw a flicker of fire in Phil's eyes. Not the fire of this world, but the fire of God. I don't know how else to explain it, but I saw it, more real than any flame I've ever seen on this earth.

I nodded my agreement as I repeated the words, "Father, forgive them."

"Phil," I continued, "if Jesus could forgive that man, there is nothing you've told us tonight that God won't forgive you of. Nothing. You've got to repent, confess these sins, turn away from them and turn totally to Christ. Do you understand?"

Phil nodded again.

I looked at the clock, then at DJ across the table from me. "We've got to pray."

We all bowed our heads and prayed out desperate prayers for Phil and against the voices. We finished, and I asked Phil what was going on.

"When you prayed," he said with wild eyes, "They said 'We're burning, we're burning.'"

I stared at Phil. "You mean the voices said that?"

He swallowed and nodded his head.

I looked at DJ and I think we both said at the same time, "We're going to pray some more."

And pray we did. We prayed the blood of Jesus over Phil and us and everyone there. Although in reality it was just a short time in prayer, it was extremely intense and I felt almost wiped out when we were done. When we finished, I looked at Phil.

He was now looking up, looking at the ceiling, or perhaps past it, I couldn't tell. He had the look in his eyes of a little child seeing fireworks for the first time. The look of a very strong, very large, yet little child. A look of wonder I will not soon forget.

"What's happening, Phil?" I asked gently.

"I feel light-headed." was all Phil could get out before a huge grin covered his face.

"Like a weight has been lifted?" I asked.

Phil nodded. "Yeah, that's it. Like a big weight has been taken off of me."

Then the sound of the loud electronic door unlocking shattered the quiet that had surrounded us. Phil and the other inmates exited the room.

"Man, that was something," DJ said as we stared at each other.

"You're not kidding," I replied, still a bit stunned at what had just taken place.

The next week Phil did not return for our study. That was about the time I started getting a few thoughts of my own about what we'd experienced. *You're so naive, you got conned big time. Phil is probably boasting about how he conned you and DJ, hook, line and sinker. You two are the laughing stock of the whole prison.*

So I started praying, "Dear God, I know You're real. And I know the blood of Jesus is real and just as powerful today as it was when He shed it on that cross. Powerful to forgive all sin, to break every stronghold. Dear God, I believe Phil was sincere. But even if he was playing a con game, that doesn't change anything about Your blood on the cross. Not a thing."

Phil didn't come back the next week either, and the battle in my mind continued. In fact, it was quite a while before Phil finally did come back. When he did, I wanted to corner him and talk to him as soon as I saw him walk through the door. However, that's not something easily done at the prison, or even advisable for that matter. So all of us sat and discussed

55

our Bible lesson for the evening.

When the study was over I planted myself squarely between Phil and the door. I realize my faith is not what it should be, so I probably shouldn't have needed to talk to Phil at all. But there was no telling when or if he'd be back. I wasn't going to let him get out of that room until I spoke with him.

Phil got up from his chair and lumbered towards the door. He was carrying a large Bible with him, and he was hugging it close to the middle of his chest. He was holding it like a big running back holds a football so no one will be able to tear it from his hands. Although the Bible was big, Phil's two huge forearms nearly covered the entire thing.

As Phil went by me he let go of the Bible with his right hand and engulfed my hand in his big paw.

"How are you doing, Phil?" I asked as he continued to walk past me.

"Oh, doing pretty good, thanks, doing okay. How about you?"

I had no desire to talk about my well-being, so I got to the point before the big man walked out the door.

"Well, what about the voices, man, what about them?" I pressed as I backpedaled to stay with him.

"Oh, them," said Phil as he stopped and tried to remember the evil things, acting as if they were ancient history. "They tried to come back. A couple of times. But they couldn't. They can't touch me now." At that Phil grinned and shook my hand again, light and life now beaming from his eyes. Then he turned and left the room, a man walking under the precious blood of the Lamb.

[K]nowing that you were not redeemed with corruptible things, like silver or gold, from your aimless conduct received by tradition from your fathers, but with the precious blood of Christ, as of a lamb without blemish and without spot (1 Peter 1:18-19).

But if we walk in the light as He is in the light, we have fellowship with one another, and the blood of Jesus Christ His Son cleanses us from all sin (1 John 1:7).

[G]iving thanks to the Father who has qualified us to be partakers of the inheritance of the saints in the light. He has delivered us from the power of darkness and conveyed us into the kingdom of the Son of His love, in whom we have redemption through His blood, the forgiveness of sins (Colossians 1:12-14).

In Him we have redemption through His blood, the forgiveness of sins, according to the riches of His grace . . . (Ephesians 1:7).

[R]emember that at that time you were separate from Christ, excluded from citizenship in Israel and foreigners to the covenants of the promise, without hope and without God in the world. But now in Christ Jesus you who once were far away have been brought near through the blood of Christ (Ephesians 2:12-13 NIV).

For it pleased the Father that in Him all the fullness should dwell, and by Him to reconcile all things to Himself, by Him, whether things on earth or things in heaven, having made peace through the blood of His cross (Colossians 1:19-20).

Then I heard a loud voice in heaven say: "Now have come the salvation and the power and the kingdom of our God, and the authority of his Christ. For the accuser of our brothers, who accuses them before our God day and night, has been hurled down. They overcame him by the blood of the Lamb and by the word of their testimony; they did not love their lives so much as to shrink from death" (Revelation 12:10-11 NIV).

[A]nd from Jesus Christ, the faithful witness, the firstborn from the dead, and the ruler over the kings of the earth. To Him who loved us and washed us from our sins in His own blood . . . (Revelation 1:5).

And they sang a new song: "You are worthy to take the scroll and to open its seals, because you were slain, and with your blood you purchased men for God from every tribe and language and people and nation" (Revelation 5:9 NIV).

But God demonstrates His own love toward us, in that while we were still sinners, Christ died for us. Much more then, having now been justified by His blood, we shall be saved from wrath through Him. For if when we were enemies we were reconciled to God through the death of His Son, much more, having been reconciled, we shall be saved by His life (Romans 5:8-10).

This righteousness from God comes through faith in Jesus Christ to all who believe. There is no difference, for all have sinned and fall short of the glory of God, and are justified freely by his grace through the redemption that came by Christ Jesus. God presented him as a sacrifice of atonement, through faith in his blood. He did this to demonstrate his justice, because in his forbearance he had left the sins committed beforehand unpunished—he did it to demonstrate his justice at the present time, so as to be just and the one who justifies those who have faith in Jesus (Romans 3:22-26 NIV).

When Christ came as high priest of the good things that are already here, he went through the greater and more perfect tabernacle that is not man-made, that is to say, not a part of this creation. He did not enter by means of the blood of goats and calves; but he entered the Most Holy Place once for all by his own blood, having obtained eternal redemption. The blood of goats and bulls and the ashes of a heifer sprinkled on those who are ceremonially unclean sanctify them so that they are outwardly clean. How much more, then, will the blood of Christ, who through the eternal Spirit offered himself unblemished to God, cleanse our consciences from acts that lead to death, so that we may serve the living God!

In fact, the law requires that nearly everything be cleansed with blood, and without the shedding of blood there is no forgiveness (Hebrews 9:11-14; 22 NIV).

"No weapon forged against you will prevail, and you will refute every tongue that accuses you. This is the heritage of the servants of the LORD, and this is their vindication from me," declares the LORD (Isaiah 54:17 NIV).

How God anointed and consecrated Jesus of Nazareth with the [Holy] Spirit and with strength and ability and power; how He went about doing good and, in particular, curing all who were harassed and oppressed by the power of the devil, for God was with Him (Acts 10:38 AMP).

— 6 —

After-Christmas Gift

Holiday commitments make it difficult for volunteers to come into the prison, but we consciously try to have at least one person show up for service during those times. So I was surprised that all of us were able to make it to the prison on this particular day, December 26. Inmates are especially appreciative when we visit them during holiday seasons, and they seem particularly open to the gospel at these times. While I learned lessons myself that night, it sobers me to think where one young man would be if we hadn't made the effort to be there on that particular evening.

It was my turn to teach, and as the men took their seats, I once again noticed the hierarchy among the prisoners in the room. Tonight the top man of the tier, Mel, decided to sit next to me in the circle of chairs. He moved his seat back a little so he could not only see me, but by turning his head he could flip his long hair over his shoulder and see everyone else in the room. And in positioning himself as he did, Mel made sure everyone else could see him as well. As he reacted to the teaching, Mel expected the other inmates to respond accordingly. As the lesson went on, Mel spent more time glaring at the prisoners who were asking questions about the birth of Jesus than looking at me. Before long, it was obvious that Mel was downright perturbed that others were taking an interest in the Bible teaching.

I'd seen Mel before, and I knew that he was involved with the occult. As he continued his intimidation efforts, I became even more determined to speak of Jesus and His awesome love and sacrifice for us. It was an intense hour, but finally we reached the part that is one of the most difficult, yet rewarding, to do.

"I'm going to give everyone here a chance to accept Jesus as Lord and Savior," I said. "Now I try my best never to embarrass anyone. I don't ask anyone to come up front or stand up or anything like that. This is a personal decision between you and God. What I'm going to do is pray a prayer to repent of your sins and accept Jesus into your life. You can use my words or use your own. God looks at your heart, not how articulate you might or might not be.

"Jesus said if you deny Me before men, I'm going to deny you before My Father in heaven. But if you acknowledge Me before men, I'll acknowledge you before My Father in heaven.

"So after I pray this prayer, I'm going to ask anyone who has accepted Christ as your Savior to just put your hand up for a moment, and then put it back down. That will be your chance to acknowledge Him before me, another man. I hope that you'll come back and we can talk about your decision another time, and let others know about it as well, but for now that's all I'm going to ask of you. This is the most precious time of your life, the most important decision you'll ever make, because it involves being forgiven, being made right with God, and it involves eternity.

"So I ask everyone here, at least out of respect for God, to just close your eyes so people can have some privacy."

Mel sat up straight and made it clear to everyone present that he'd be watching them no matter what I said. I saw the other men bow their heads and close their eyes.

"Even if you don't respect God or me for that matter," I continued, "then out of respect for the others in this room, I ask you to close your eyes so people can have some privacy."

Mel smirked as he glared at me from a few feet away.

"Dear Jesus," I began as I did my best to ignore Mel, "I confess to You right now that I am a sinner. I take full responsibility for my sins. I believe You died on the cross for me and that You rose from the dead and are alive today. Wash me now in Your precious blood, and save me from my sins. Be the Lord and Savior of my life. I give my life to You now. Thank You for hearing me, and thank You for forgiving me."

Mel continued staring at me as I deliberately looked over his head, hoping his intimidation had not been enough to deter all in the room.

"Now if anyone here prayed that for the first time, please just raise your hand so I can see it," I stated.

A young man's hand shot up about as high as he could reach. And he held it up there for quite some time, knowing full well that Mel had to see him. Yet he was not ashamed.

Mel was so sure that no one would respond that he lingered a moment staring at me, smirk intact, before he turned his head to look at the group of men sitting to his right. He did a double-take as he realized his bullying tactics had failed. I saw his long hair do a quick flip as he whipped his head around a second time and bored holes with his eyes into the young man who dared to defy him.

"Okay, you can put your hands down now," I said as I silently gave thanks to God. I sensed the rejoicing of the other volunteers as they knew from my words that at least one prisoner had gone from death to life right there in our midst.

The service was over shortly afterward, and Mel huffed his way out of the room.

"We need to pray for that kid who accepted Christ," we agreed when all the inmates had left. "He's going to catch it good when he gets back to the tier. He's got a lot of guts to do that with Mel glaring at him."

As we walked out of the main building that night, we came to the first of two fences. I was the last in our group walking out as a myriad of emotions played in my mind. We had just celebrated the birth of the Savior of the world the day before on Christmas, and now we got to celebrate another birth, a new birth, the next day.

Somehow, God had allowed me to be a part of this rescue operation. I felt humbled to my toes and yet elated with gratitude and joy. I looked up at the razor wire on top of the two fence lines running parallel around the prison about fifteen feet apart from each other.

I feel like I could just jump over both of these fences right now if I tried, I thought. Then I looked around. *Of course, if I did, some of the officers watching would probably get a little excited. Best to just walk through the gates like the rest of the guys.*

As we walked through the second gate, I replayed in my mind the moment when the young man accepted Christ. I recalled how he held his hand up as high as he could and how Mel had reacted. *Mel whipped his head around so fast I bet he about got whiplash,'* I chuckled to myself smugly. I had just closed the gate behind me and was about to step away from it when I received a rebuke from God that rocked me.

"You are not wrestling against flesh and blood in this place; you are wrestling against spirits and principalities of darkness in the spiritual realm. I get no pleasure in the death of the wicked but that the wicked would turn from their ways and live."

The heavy metal gate clanked shut behind me as my left foot touched the ground. I stopped and stood still, stunned at what I had heard. I looked down the sidewalk as the rest of the volunteers continued on toward their cars, chatting with each other as they went. They had not heard what I just did. No one else heard at all.

I grabbed the railing next to the sidewalk to steady myself. Then I looked back through the layers of fence at the prison, the dampness of the cold winter night pressing in around me. "Dear God," I whispered, "will there ever come a time when I am done with this cursed pride of mine? You hung on that cross as much for Mel and that young man who accepted You tonight as You did for me. Oh God, forgive me."

I prayed for Mel right then and there, and still do as the Lord leads. I haven't seen him nor the young man who accepted Christ that night for many years, and don't know if either or both are still in prison or back on the streets again. I am grateful for the vital lesson I learned from God that night. And I am very grateful for the young man who had the courage to raise his hand towards heaven to reach up toward God, no matter what it might cost him. A young man born again, a birthday celebration the day after Christmas!

Jesus answered and said to him, "Most assuredly, I
say to you, unless one is born again, he cannot see the
kingdom of God.

65

"And as Moses lifted up the serpent in the wilderness, even so must the Son of Man be lifted up, that whoever believes in Him should not perish but have eternal life. For God so loved the world that He gave His only begotten Son, that whoever believes in Him should not perish but have everlasting life. For God did not send His Son into the world to condemn the world, but that the world through Him might be saved" (John 3:3, 14-17).

Therefore, if anyone is in Christ, he is a new creation; old things have passed away; behold, all things have become new (2 Corinthians 5:17).

That if you confess with your mouth, "Jesus is Lord," and believe in your heart that God raised him from the dead, you will be saved. For it is with your heart that you believe and are justified, and it is with your mouth that you confess and are saved (Romans 10:9-10 NIV).

For we do not wrestle against flesh and blood, but against principalities, against powers, against the rulers of the darkness of this age, against spiritual hosts of wickedness in the heavenly places (Ephesians 6:12).

Whatever happens, conduct yourselves in a manner worthy of the gospel of Christ . . . (Philippians 1:27 NIV).

The Lord is not slack concerning His promise, as some count slackness, but is longsuffering toward us, not willing that any should perish but that all should come to repentance (2 Peter 3:9).

Let this mind be in you which was also in Christ Jesus, who, being in the form of God, did not consider it robbery to be equal with God, but made Himself of no reputation, taking the form of a bondservant, and coming in the likeness of men. And being found in appearance as a man, He humbled Himself and became obedient to the point of death, even the death of the cross. Therefore God also has highly exalted Him and given Him the name which is above every name, that at the name of Jesus every knee should bow, of those in heaven, and of those on earth, and of those under the earth, and that every tongue should confess that Jesus Christ is Lord, to the glory of God the Father (Philippians 2:5-11).

As God's partners, we beg you not to reject this marvelous message of God's great kindness. For God says, "At just the right time, I heard you. On the day of salvation, I helped you." Indeed, God is ready to help you right now. Today is the day of salvation (2 Corinthians 6:1-2 NLT)

Say to them, "As surely as I live, declares the Sovereign LORD, I take no pleasure in the death of the wicked, but rather that they turn from their ways and live. Turn! Turn from your evil ways . . ." (Ezekiel 33:11 NIV).

—7—

The Name Above Every Name

Jasper was another one of those quiet young men who looked far too young and scared to be in maximum security. He attended our Bible studies faithfully, and sincerely seemed to want to change his ways and do something good with his life. However, as the months went on, it was obvious he was getting more and more distraught.

One day when only a few other inmates were around, he spoke to us in a quiet voice. "I'm supposed to be getting out soon, in a couple of months. And I'm in big trouble and need help. It's the drugs. I know I'm going back to the same place, the same friends I used to have on the outside. I don't want to do drugs anymore, I honestly don't. But I'm just not that strong. I know what's going to happen when I get out. I don't ever want to come back into this place again, not ever. But my friends are going to be there, and I know what's going to happen when I see them again."

Jasper looked like a deer in the headlights as he continued. "I'm starting to crave them again, the drugs. 'Romancing the stone' we call it. I don't want to, but I find myself thinking about them every moment of the day. It takes about all I've got to fight the thoughts off, and I don't know how much longer I'll be able to do it. And now I'm even starting to dream about them at night. I can't control my dreams. They're starting to consume me again, just like before, just the same way as before. I need help; I don't know how much more of this I can take. And when I get out. . . ."

The four of us volunteers looked at each other. Although I have enough weaknesses of my own to sink a boat, by the grace of God I've never been addicted to drugs. I could only imagine what Jasper was fighting. However, there was no doubt the addiction was real and already the drugs were bringing destruction into his life once again. We did the only thing we knew to do as we bowed our heads.

"Dear God, You've heard Jasper's words and You know his heart. Jesus, Your Name is above every name that's ever been named. Far above, and that includes drug addiction. So in Your Name we pray that You remove this craving for the drugs from Jasper. Set him free, totally and completely. May he never do drugs again or even desire them; may they be repulsive to him."

The next week as we gathered again for our Bible study, I had forgotten about this event. I'm pretty dull at times, but just as we began the session, the Lord prompted me to say something as I looked at Jasper. "Wait, before we start, last week we prayed about Jasper and his thoughts about the drugs. Where are things at with that?" I asked him.

Jasper looked at me as his eyes nearly bugged out of his head. Then his jaw dropped, and he started to get choked up.

"I . . . oh man," he began. "Oh man," Jasper struggled as

his face got red and his eyes began to cloud over. He fought hard not to show his emotions but it was a losing battle. He stared at me.

"I haven't thought about drugs since you guys prayed last week. Not at all. Not once in a whole week. Not once!" he managed to get out as he blinked back tears. "Not once, not even one time. Not in my dreams or while I was awake."

Then a wide grin spread across Jasper's face as he looked at each of us. "Not once," he repeated. "I can make it! I'm going to be able to make it! Oh, thank God, I'm going to be able to make it!"

* * *

Some years later, another man came to our study with another area of difficulty but basically the same problem.

"There's some guys that are giving me trouble," Frank began. "I've been known to get real mad at times. Real mad, like out of control. Now I don't want to do anything wrong here. You guys know I've been reading my Bible and studying and all. I want to do what's right in God's eyes, what He wants me to do. That's really what's in my heart. But a couple of guys are giving me a hard time. And now about all I can think about is how I'm going to hurt them. They may be able to hurt me once, but they won't the second time. They won't beat me in the end. I've been in here a long time, and I know how to do this kind of stuff. They'll pay in the end. They won't win.

"I want to do what's right for God, but now all I can think about is how I'm going to hurt these guys. And when I start thinking about it, I start getting mad. I mean real mad, like I can't control it or something. It's what I'm starting to think about all the time now. I can't seem to think about anything else. They shouldn't be messing with me like they are. I don't want to hurt anyone, and I told them to leave me alone. But if they keep it up, I may get so angry that I can't control it. And down on the tier, I can't get away from them; they're always in my face, always taunting me every chance they get. I can't think about anything else but hurting both those guys."

Even though it had been a while, my mind went back to Jasper and how his thoughts were getting beyond his control. We prayed again.

"Dear God, we ask you right now to remove this anger from Frank. We just come against this anger in the Name of Jesus. Lord, we ask You to remove it now, cast it away so that it will not come to Frank's mind again. He says he wants to live for You and doesn't want to hurt anyone or get out of control with his anger anymore, and You know his heart, God. Help him in every way concerning this situation, God. We pray this in Jesus' Name."

The next week the same men were back at our Bible study. I was relieved to see that it didn't look like Frank had been in any fights recently. I asked him how it was going with his anger issues. Frank's jaw dropped as he squinted up his eyes and stared at me, but he didn't say anything. Bill, one of the other prisoners sitting next to him spoke up.

"Frank, you remember what we all prayed about last week? Remember how you were thinking about how you were going to tear those two guys up who've been giving you grief all this time? That's what he's talking about."

Frank looked at Bill, then back at me. "I know I've got an anger problem, but I don't even remember what you're talking about. I'm not mad at anybody right now. Are you sure that was me?"

Bill started to laugh. "Yeah, man, it was you, alright." Then he looked at me.

72

"I know this guy," Bill said as he pointed his thumb at Frank, sounding rather astounded at the whole thing. "He's not making this up. We're on the same tier together. He's not been into it with anyone this week."

"Do you believe God can do something like that for someone who calls on Jesus, who calls out to Him to change his life?" I asked them both.

Bill smiled wide while Frank still looked puzzled at the whole conversation. "I do now," Bill said slowly, "I do now."

Frank shrugged his shoulders, "Yeah, I believe God can do it, but are you guys sure you're talking about me?"

Ah Lord GOD! Behold, You have made the heavens and the earth by Your great power and by Your outstretched arm! Nothing is too difficult for You . . . (Jeremiah 32:17 NASB).

Therefore I also, after I heard of your faith in the Lord Jesus and your love for all the saints, do not cease to give thanks for you, making mention of you in my prayers: that the God of our Lord Jesus Christ, the Father of glory, may give to you the spirit of wisdom and revelation in the knowledge of Him, the eyes of your understanding being enlightened; that you may know what is the hope of His calling, what are the riches of the glory of His inheritance in the saints, and what is the exceeding greatness of His power toward us who believe, according to the working of His mighty power which He worked in Christ when He raised Him from the dead and seated Him at His right hand in the heavenly places, far above all principality and power and might and dominion, and every name that is named, not only in this age but also in that which is to come. And He put all things under

His feet, and gave Him to be head over all things to the church, which is His body, the fullness of Him who fills all in all. (Ephesians 1:15-23).

Therefore God also has highly exalted Him and given Him the name which is above every name, that at the name of Jesus every knee should bow, of those in heaven, and of those on earth, and of those under the earth, and that every tongue should confess that Jesus Christ is Lord, to the glory of God the Father (Philippians 2: 9-11).

If then you have been raised with Christ [to a new life, thus sharing His resurrection from the dead], aim at and seek the [rich, eternal treasures] that are above, where Christ is, seated at the right hand of God. And set your minds and keep them set on what is above (the higher things), not on the things that are on the earth (Colossians 3:1-2 AMP).

I have told you these things, so that in Me you may have [perfect] peace and confidence. In the world you have tribulation and trials and distress and frustration; but be of good cheer [take courage; be confident, certain, undaunted]! For I have overcome the world. [I have deprived it of power to harm you and have conquered it for you] (John 16:33 AMP).

No, in all these things we are more than conquerors through him who loved us. For I am convinced that neither death nor life, neither angels nor demons, neither the present nor the future, nor any powers, neither height nor depth, nor anything else in all creation, will be able to separate us from the love of God that is in Christ Jesus our Lord (Romans 8:37-39 NIV).

Do you not know that your body is a temple of the Holy Spirit, who is in you, whom you have received from God? You are not your own; you were bought at a price. Therefore honor God with your body (1 Corinthians 6:19-20 NIV).

His divine power has given us everything we need for life and godliness through our knowledge of him who called us by his own glory and goodness. Through these he has given us his very great and precious promises, so that through them you may participate in the divine nature and escape the corruption in the world caused by evil desires (2 Peter 1:3-4 NIV).

Finally, brethren, whatever things are true, whatever things are noble, whatever things are just, whatever things are pure, whatever things are lovely, whatever things are of good report, if there is any virtue and if there is anything praiseworthy—meditate on these things (Philippians 4:8).

—8—

The Power of Forgiveness

As many followers of Christ can attest, Jesus' command to forgive can at times be the most difficult thing that He tells us to do. Yet if we are obedient, it can perhaps be the most freeing as well. Jesus purchased our forgiveness and freedom through His death on the cross. Forgiveness is an integral part of the gospel of Christ, and discussions on the need to forgive others consistently garner some of the most encouraging remarks from prisoners who are open to the truth of Jesus' words.

Recently I've felt led to teach about forgiveness on a regular basis at the prison. I often use some of the same Scriptures I read a few months earlier, bringing out some of the points of which I myself need to be reminded. Many times inmates who usually don't participate in the Bible study will take part in these discussions. After the study is over, it seems at least one of the men will come to me privately and tell me how much he needed this study on this particular night.

One inmate shared an experience about the power of forgiveness that has stayed with me for a long time. We had been discussing Jesus' response to Peter in Matthew 18. The fisherman asked the Lord how often he had to forgive someone who offended him.

"There are a few points I'd like to bring out about what Jesus says here," I stated. "The kingdom of God is about forgiveness. Without being forgiven, none of us are going to make it into God's Kingdom. I hope that everyone here understands that our forgiveness is not something we can earn on our own. It is through Jesus and His sacrifice for us on the cross, being washed clean of our sins through His precious blood. The guy who was forgiven in this story had no way of ever paying back what he owed. It is the same with us trying to pay back or work off the debt of the sin we've committed in our lives.

"The Bible says we've all sinned, and if we're honest with ourselves, we know that's true. And the Bible says we are helpless to pay it back; we can't earn it or do anything on our own to pay it back short of our paying for it by spending eternity in hell. Or we can call out to the One Who has already made the payment by taking the punishment for our sins so we don't have to. That's exactly what Jesus did when He went to the cross. If we've called on Him, since we've been forgiven of so much more than we could ever pay for, we must forgive those who do wrong against us.

"Also, when this guy didn't forgive his fellow man, it made the master very angry. We may have lots of folks angry with us: our family, our celly, the judge, the officer on duty tonight, whoever. None of that's good. But there is Someone we really don't want angry with us, and that's God. Something very, very bad happens to our relationship with God when we don't forgive others. As Christ forgave us, we have to forgive

78

others. When we don't forgive, we grieve the Holy Spirit. And look at this part of the parable; the first man had a chance to show someone else the compassion of the master, but he didn't do it. You and I have a chance to show the world what Jesus is like when we forgive. The world says 'Get even, or get "one up" on someone.' Jesus tells us to forgive. It's a chance to show Christ to others. And by doing that, we can stop the destruction that Satan wants to bring. You can stop his plan totally. Through Christ, you have the power to defeat the enemy."

One of the inmates spoke up. "That very thing you just said happened to me once, the thing about defeating the enemy of our souls by forgiving someone," Mick stated solemnly. "In fact, it saved my life."

"What happened to you?" I asked.

Mick thought a moment as if deciding if he should share his experience or not. It may have been the first time he ever did. Mick took a deep breath. "Well," he continued softly, "one time my brother stabbed me in the back of my head with a knife. Knocked me right down on the floor. He was coming after me, coming to kill me. He was all strung out on junk. I rolled over on my back and grabbed the back of my head. There was blood coming out, going everywhere. I saw him coming at me with the knife. He was right over me, and he was just crazy. I looked right at him and said 'I forgive you, Fred.'

"When I did, it was like something snapped in him. He stopped and sort of wavered a bit, as if he were stunned by my words. Then he looked at the knife and at me, at what he'd done. He dropped the knife and called 911. They got me to the hospital, and obviously, I made it. It was close, real close. But I really felt that I forgave my brother right then; that's the only way I could have said what I did. And when he heard me say that I forgave him, he stopped right in his tracks. Everything stopped – the anger – the craziness. It was like he changed in an instant."

"I've heard of powerful stories of forgiveness, but I don't think I've ever heard of anything quite like what you just told me," I said. "Not ever."

Mick nodded his agreement. "Forgiveness is powerful, man. I'm living proof of it. What it says here in the Bible is right. At the moment I told Fred that I forgave him, I knew Jesus was there. I had faith in Him. Even if I died, I'd be okay. I just wanted Fred to know I forgave him."

For he has rescued us from the one who rules in the kingdom of darkness, and he has brought us into the Kingdom of his dear Son. God has purchased our freedom with his blood and has forgiven all our sins (Colossians 1:13-14 NLT).

For You, Lord, are good, and ready to forgive, And abundant in mercy to all those who call upon You (Psalm 86:5).

Do not let any unwholesome talk come out of your mouths, but only what is helpful for building others up according to their needs, that it may benefit those who listen. And do not grieve the Holy Spirit of God, with whom you were sealed for the day of redemption. Get rid of all bitterness, rage and anger, brawling and slander, along with every form of malice. Be kind and compassionate to one another, forgiving each other, just as in Christ God forgave you (Ephesians 4:29-32 NIV).

Therefore, as the elect of God, holy and beloved, put on tender mercies, kindness, humility, meekness, longsuffering; bearing with one another, and forgiving one another, if anyone has a complaint against another; even as Christ forgave you, so you also must do (Colossians 3:12-13).

"In this manner, therefore, pray: Our Father in heaven, Hallowed be Your name. Your kingdom come. Your will be done On earth as it is in heaven. Give us this day our daily bread. And forgive us our debts, As we forgive our debtors. And do not lead us into temptation, But deliver us from the evil one. For Yours is the kingdom and the power and the glory forever. Amen. For if you forgive men their trespasses, your heavenly Father will also forgive you. But if you do not forgive men their trespasses, neither will your Father forgive your trespasses" (Matthew 6:9-15).

"You have heard that it was said, 'You shall love your neighbor and hate your enemy.' But I say to you, love your enemies, bless those who curse you, do good to those who hate you, and pray for those who spitefully use you and persecute you, that you may be sons of your Father in heaven; for He makes His sun rise on the evil and on the good, and sends rain on the just and on the unjust. For if you love those who love you, what reward have you? Do not even the tax collectors do the same? And if you greet your brethren only, what do you do more than others? Do not even the tax collectors do so? Therefore you shall be perfect, just as your Father in heaven is perfect" (Matthew 5:43-48).

So Jesus answered and said to them, "Have faith in God. For assuredly, I say to you, whoever says to this mountain, 'Be removed and be cast into the sea,' and does not doubt in his heart, but believes that those things he says will be done, he will have whatever he says. Therefore I say to you, whatever things you ask when you pray, believe that you receive them, and you will have them. And whenever you stand praying, if you have anything against anyone, forgive him, that your Father in heaven may also forgive you your trespasses. But if you do not forgive, neither will your Father in heaven forgive your trespasses" (Mark 11:22-26).

Then Peter came to Him and said, "Lord, how often shall my brother sin against me, and I forgive him? Up to seven times?" Jesus said to him, "I do not say to you, up to seven times, but up to seventy times seven. Therefore the kingdom of heaven is like a certain king who wanted to settle accounts with his servants. And when he had begun to settle accounts, one was brought to him who owed him ten thousand talents. But as he was not able to pay, his master commanded that he be sold, with his wife and children and all that he had, and that payment be made. The servant therefore fell down before him, saying, 'Master, have patience with me, and I will pay you all.' Then the master of that servant was moved with compassion, released him, and forgave him the debt. But that servant went out and found one of his fellow servants who owed him a hundred denarii; and he laid hands on him and took him by the throat, saying, 'Pay me what you owe!' So his fellow servant fell down at his feet and begged him, saying, 'Have patience with me, and I will pay you all.' And he would not, but went and threw him into prison till he should pay the debt. So when his fellow servants saw what had been done, they were very grieved, and came and told their master all that had been done. Then his master, after he had called him, said to him, 'You wicked servant! I forgave you all that debt because you begged me. 'Should you not also have had compassion on your fellow servant, just as I had pity on you?' And his master was angry, and delivered him to the torturers until he should pay all that was due to him.

So My heavenly Father also will do to you if each of you, from his heart, does not forgive his brother his trespasses" (Matthew 18:21-35).

—9—

The Broken and the Brokenhearted

Many correctional officers whom I've met in the prison sincerely want to see inmates change for the better. They want inmates to make constructive contributions to society once they finish their sentences and return to the streets. There are surely secular programs within the correctional system designed to help inmates do just that. Yet due to various constraints, those within the system who wish to speak about God are limited in what they can or cannot say regarding Him. However, I once had an officer tell me that Jesus meant so much to him that he didn't care if he did lose his job; he was going to speak about Him anyway.

Over the years, I've caught a little grief for my belief in Christ. I have had some interesting comments aimed my way for going into the prison system. Some have asked me if I'm not afraid for my safety. In fact, after one night's Bible study, a fight broke out with about fifteen to twenty inmates from maximum security—and three of us volunteers in the room.

I think I aged a few years that evening, but God is good, and His protection is and was quite real that night. The two other volunteers and I had some interesting conversations following that session about what each of us did during the brawl. Personally, I sought out the biggest inmate in the room, a man built much like a refrigerator.

I was taking a gamble because the man had only said about three words since I'd met him, and I didn't know if he liked me or not. I stood next to him and shouted over all the yelling and cursing that I was sure glad he was there that night and that I really appreciated him coming to the Bible studies. He looked at me as if I were crazy, but no one ever did take a swing at him – or at me – during the entire incident.

* * *

The Lord has revealed interesting facets of the gospel while I've ministered in the prison. Occasionally an inmate will come to a session and tell us that he was healed of something that we'd prayed for earlier. I specifically remember inmates reporting that they've been healed of sore backs and arms, although the reports we hear have not been limited to just these things. While I have no way to verify this medically, the inmates are grateful nonetheless.

Sometimes the Holy Spirit empowers the gospel to break through the walls put up by even the strongest of inmates. Recently during a Bible study, we presented the gospel and a gruff, burly inmate named Mark began to weep uncontrollably.

Until that day, Mark had been very reserved and quiet. He had built a wall around his emotions, but that evening it came crashing down before our eyes. The big man wept and wept as he held his face in his hands. When Mark finally managed to stop crying, he haltingly told us of a time when he was on the outside and another man, Bill, had shown unexpected kindness toward him. When no one else seemed to care if Mark was dead or alive, Bill took care of him. Mark went on and on about how kind Bill had been, and how he'd had Mark over to his house at Thanksgiving when Mark was all alone.

Then Mark related to us how he'd just found out that Bill had died very suddenly and unexpectedly. Mark said that he himself had recently accepted Jesus as his personal Savior and Lord but he had never told Bill about his decision. Mark had had the chance, but he never told Bill about what a difference Christ was making in his own life.

Now Bill was dead, and Mark was beside himself with grief since he'd never told his friend about Christ. Mark knew Bill was facing an eternity in hell if he hadn't called on Jesus.

Mark's story was a very sobering reminder for all of us in the room to take advantage of any opportunities God gives us. Opportunities to share what Jesus has done for us with those people we care about and hopefully with a lot of others as well.

Another aspect of the gospel has made me cautiously optimistic about an extremely sensitive issue. We volunteers seldom bring the matter up, but when a *prisoner* broaches the subject, then something powerful takes place. This is especially true if an inmate who is high up in the prison hierarchy starts the conversation.

This aspect concerns repentance and the realization of the pain inmates have caused others. It involves taking responsibility for their actions and not blaming something or someone else for their failures. There seems to be an understanding of the lives and hearts that have been shattered and broken due to the inmates' past actions. I know this is not an easy thing to acknowledge regardless of where one lives. However, I believe when this happens, it can only be attributed to God, especially when it takes place among inmates living inside the razor wire.

Once in a great while an inmate will announce that it is time for him and everyone else present to pray for the victims of their crimes. When this occurs, many, if not all of the other inmates agree wholeheartedly. Then the prayers lifted up by the inmates are both poignant and humbling. The prayers reflect deep and heartfelt repentance, asking for healing and freedom for their victims, freedom from pain and the past trauma and destruction caused by the inmates themselves. The men seem to comprehend that only Jesus can bring about this healing, for He alone is able.

To God be all the glory, now and forever.

The LORD is close to the brokenhearted and saves those who are crushed in spirit (Psalm 34:18 NIV).

He heals the brokenhearted And binds up their wounds (Psalm 147:3).

He is despised and rejected by men, A Man of sorrows and acquainted with grief. And we hid, as it were, our faces from Him; He was despised, and we did not esteem Him. Surely He has borne our griefs And carried our sorrows; Yet we esteemed Him stricken, Smitten by God, and afflicted. But He was wounded for our transgressions, He was bruised for our iniquities; The chastisement for our peace was upon Him, And by His stripes we are healed (Isaiah 53:3-5).

When He had come down from the mountain, great multitudes followed Him. And behold, a leper came and worshiped Him, saying, "Lord, if You are willing, You can make me clean." Then Jesus put out His hand and touched him, saying, "I am willing; be cleansed." Immediately his leprosy was cleansed (Matthew 8:1-3).

This fulfilled the word of the Lord through the prophet Isaiah, who said, "He took our sicknesses and removed our diseases" (Matthew 8:17 NLT).

By faith in the name of Jesus, this man whom you see and know was made strong. It is Jesus' name and the faith that comes through him that has given this complete healing to him, as you can all see (Acts 3:16 NIV).

It is the Spirit who gives life; the flesh profits nothing. The words that I speak to you are spirit, and they are life (John 6:63).

But if the Spirit of Him who raised Jesus from the dead dwells in you, He who raised Christ from the dead will also give life to your mortal bodies through His Spirit who dwells in you (Romans 8:11).

For to this you were called, because Christ also suffered for us, leaving us an example, that you should follow His steps: "Who committed no sin, Nor was deceit found in His mouth" who, when He was reviled, did not revile in return; when He suffered, He did not threaten, but committed Himself to Him who judges righteously; who Himself bore our sins in His own body on the tree, that we, having died to sins, might live for righteousness—by whose stripes you were healed (1 Peter 2:21-24).

This is all the more urgent, for you know how late it is; time is running out. Wake up, for our salvation is nearer now than when we first believed. The night is almost gone; the day of salvation will soon be here. So remove your dark deeds like dirty clothes, and put on the shining armor of right living (Romans 13:11-12 NLT).

Have you not known? Have you not heard? The everlasting God, the LORD, The Creator of the ends of the earth, Neither faints nor is weary. His understanding is unsearchable. He gives power to the weak, And to those who have no might He increases strength. Even the youths shall faint and be weary, And the young men shall utterly fall, But those who wait on the LORD Shall renew their strength; They shall mount up with wings like eagles, They shall run and not be weary, They shall walk and not faint (Isaiah 40:28-31).

Teach us to realize the brevity of life, so that we may grow in wisdom (Psalm 90:12 NLT).

Praise the LORD, O my soul; all my inmost being, praise his holy name. Praise the LORD, O my soul, and forget not all his benefits- who forgives all your sins and heals all your diseases, who redeems your life from the pit and crowns you with love and compassion, who satisfies your desires with good things so that your youth is renewed like the eagle's (Psalm 103:1-5 NIV).

Nothing in all creation is hidden from God's sight. Everything is uncovered and laid bare before the eyes of him to whom we must give account. Therefore, since we have a great high priest who has gone through the heavens, Jesus the Son of God, let us hold firmly to the faith we profess. For we do not have a high priest who is unable to sympathize with our weaknesses, but we have one who has been tempted in every way, just as we are—yet was without sin. Let us then approach the throne of grace with confidence, so that we may receive mercy and find grace to help us in our time of need (Hebrews 4:13-16 NIV).

He who dwells in the shelter of the Most High will rest in the shadow of the Almighty. I will say of the LORD, "He is my refuge and my fortress, my God, in whom I trust." Surely he will save you from the fowler's snare and from the deadly pestilence. He will cover you with his feathers, and under his wings you will find refuge; his faithfulness will be your shield and rampart. You will not fear the terror of night, nor the arrow that flies by day, nor the pestilence that stalks in the darkness, nor the plague that destroys at midday. A thousand may fall at your side, ten thousand at your right hand, but it will not come near you. You will only observe with your eyes and see the punishment of the wicked. If you make the Most High your dwelling—even the LORD, who is my refuge—then no harm will befall you, no disaster will come near your tent. For he will command his angels concerning you to guard you in all your ways; they will lift you up in their hands, so that you will not strike your foot against a stone. You will tread upon the lion and the cobra; you will trample the great lion and the serpent. "Because he loves me," says the LORD, "I will rescue him; I will protect him, for he acknowledges my name. He will call upon me, and I will answer him; I will be with him in trouble, I will deliver him and honor him. With long life will I satisfy him and show him my salvation" (Psalm 91 NIV).

—10—

Our Only Hope

I recently spoke with a former inmate who is currently living in a new community. Before his release, Julius had attended many of our prison Bible studies.

When asked if he had ever considered the possibility of prison in his younger years, his response was immediate.

"Never, no. We used to even joke about it. I used to be a police officer before going to prison. When I was in the police academy, we would joke about it, about what would happen if we ever went to prison. 'We'd probably be the tough guys,' we joked. 'We'd probably be recruited to be guards.' Just silly thoughts, it never entered my mind that I could ever land in prison."

In his younger years, Julius had been in the Marines as well. "I was full of pride, full of myself. I thought I didn't need church and I didn't need the Bible." However, his wife accepted Christ as her Lord and Savior, and she told Julius if he didn't change his ways, things weren't going to work between them. She asked him to come to church with her and he grudgingly agreed to go. What he saw shocked him.

"This was a huge church," said Julius, his hands spread out wide. "I was overwhelmed. People there were shaking my hand, telling me they were glad to see me. I didn't know these people. They start worshiping and pretty soon, I see people lifting their hands, people crying. So I asked my wife, 'What the heck! Why are they crying? 'Well, they're just worshiping," she said, so I asked, 'Why are their hands in the air?' 'That's a sign of surrender,' she said. 'That's weird.' I told her.

"Looking back, I can see how God was trying to get my attention. I was living in LA and driving to Camp Pendleton each weekend, which is about 120 miles one way. I used to drive fast to work, and there'd be a slow car in front of me. And it would have a bumper sticker from that church on it. I'd want to pass and I'd get angry. LA traffic, all those cars, and I've got *this* one in front of me. Then I'd look over once I got around them, and I'd want to curse at them. But when I looked at them, they were all happy in the car. Happy and smiling, in LA traffic! How could I get angry with that? So I'd just take off around them.

"Over the weeks, I kept seeing these bumper stickers everywhere. And when I get close to the camp, there is this two-lane road, and I'm going like twenty miles per hour behind this eighteen-wheeler and I'm late. And right on the back of this huge truck is the name of this church. Now I get to stare at it as I'm driving behind it. I went back and told my wife, 'Those people from that church, they're really getting on my nerves. Drive slow, always happy. Weird.'"

As time went on Julius kept going to church. He said that he heard some very good preachers while there, and he did get to hear the gospel—the good news of Jesus Christ—presented as well. Yet he felt he didn't need to personally apply what was being said. Even though his home life was starting to crumble, he still believed there was nothing wrong with him. After all, he was in the military and serving his country. He believed he had it all under control.

Julius' wife, however, had had all she could take of his pride and his ungodly lifestyle. Finally, she told Julius that if he didn't change, they couldn't be together anymore. So Julius moved out of their home.

"I knew something needed to change, not because I *wanted* to change, but because I didn't want to lose my wife. So I kept going to church. I didn't go with honest intentions, I just thought, *Well, I'll play the game.* I remember putting my finger in my wife's face and saying; 'You will never see me carrying a Bible. You'll never see me like these people— worshiping – at church. They are just weird.' I think at that moment, God may have said 'Oh, really?' Then we moved to another state and I got in trouble."

I asked Julius what he felt when he realized he was going to prison.

"I was out on bail. My parents were with me when I walked into court. My wife was there with a friend. My wife was crying. We sat in the back. They finally called my case, so I went up before the judge. I remember when I went up there I was still thinking that I was just going to get a slap on the wrist. They're going to say, 'You'd better not do that again.'"

Julius paused a moment. "I remember the prosecutor saying, 'This guy was a police officer, he was a Marine, he should have known better. He needs to be made an example of.' And I felt the hairs on the back of my neck go up. I started getting nervous. But I thought, *They just want to sound good in front of the judge because that's what prosecutors do.*

95

"My attorney stood up and said that I had served my country honorably and all that. But I was watching the judge, and he had an expressionless face and I thought, *Oh boy*.

"The first words out of the judge's mouth were: 'It doesn't matter what he's done in his past, what matters is why we're here in this court today. I agree with the prosecution, we need to make an example out of him.' I knew that the next words out of his mouth were going to change my life. He said; 'I sentence you to two years in prison and eight years indeterminate.' I remember thinking that this was a long time."

Julius then quietly recalled what happened next. "I remember I turned around and looked at my mom. She was weeping. I felt sad because I had hurt my mom. I felt sad because my ex-wife—she was still my wife at that time – was crying. And I could see the disappointment in my father's eyes. I felt ashamed, disappointed in myself, having been so selfish to hurt the people that I loved the most."

I asked Julius if he was afraid for his own safety after he was sentenced to prison.

"No, not at first," said Julius. "But when I got sentenced and walked into the jail, that's when it hit me. Because when you walk in, you have to walk in front of the cells. All the guys in the cells line up against the doors to see who's coming to jail. They can see who got sentenced and who got set free. And everybody saw me; they saw the handcuffs still on me. Everybody's expression was like; "Hey, isn't that . . ." and I thought, *I was just wearing a badge here a couple of weeks ago. Now I'm going to be put inside with these guys? I hope I didn't make anybody mad, I hope I didn't treat anybody wrong.*

The warden of the jail knew they couldn't put Julius in with the other inmates. He had him separated from everyone else initially, at least for his time in the jail. However, as Julius

96

sat there alone, fear of what was coming next struck him. He knew he'd soon be leaving the jail and heading to prison.

I asked him if he remembered what that first day in prison was like.

Julius closed his eyes for a moment as he recalled the day. "I remember all the razor wire when I got off the bus. When I went to boot camp, there was a bunch of yelling and there was that fear of the unknown, and here was that feeling again. Just seeing the guards, seeing the razor wire, the dogs, the towers. All these sights that I'd seen in movies and read about in books. Now I was living it, I was coming to live in this place. I knew there were some bad people in this place."

Once at the prison, Julius was put into protective custody where other inmates couldn't easily get to him. "There were other prisoners who recognized me. I had twenty-three hours a day when I was in a nine by nine cell. I had two books: the Bible and another book, I don't even remember what the other book was. I was lying there and thinking about my life, and I started weeping.

"I remembered some of the prayers I'd heard, some of the sermons that I'd heard at that church. I remembered the pastor saying that God loves you and He can create new creations. I took the little bits and pieces that I'd heard, and I prayed. I got on my knees. I don't know why I got on my knees, I'd never really seen anyone pray on their knees, but I got on my knees. I guess it was a prayer. I said 'God, I'm sorry for what I did. I'm sorry I messed things up the way I did. I'm sorry that I hurt people. I don't know how this prayer thing works, but I really need You now. Come into my life.'"

Julius then slid towards the front of his chair as he continued, "I opened the Bible. No one taught me how to read the Bible, so I just opened it to Genesis 1:1: 'In the beginning, God created the heavens and the earth.' And I read through the whole Bible in two months.

"I didn't know what they were talking about in, like, Leviticus. I didn't know what this was about. I closed the Bible, and I said 'God, what did I just read? Will You help me understand what all this means?' So for whatever reason, I started reading the book of Matthew again. Then I got transferred to another prison and couldn't bring that Bible with me. I didn't know they were all over the place at the next prison."

I asked Julius what was the most difficult thing for him in prison.

"Because I had the military structure in my mind, dealing with that aspect of things didn't bother me. You know, be up at this time, be at lunch at this time. But the selfishness was constant, people complaining about everything, complaining about the guards, the food. I realized that I was the one who put me here. But a lot of others just wanted to blame someone else for where they were. Not everybody, but enough."

* * *

I remembered something that took place when Julius was still in prison and attending one of our Bible studies. Another inmate stated decisively that since there was so much cursing and swearing down on the tier where he lived, no one could possibly spend much time down there and not speak the same way. He said it was impossible not to curse all the time if you lived where they lived, apparently trying to justify his own foul mouth.

Then something unusual happened. Another inmate pointed at Julius and said that *he* was able to do it, so it had to be possible. I saw other inmates nod their agreement. Not one of the inmates in the group argued the point, so it was obvious they were telling the truth about Julius' language while away from the Bible study.

* * *

I asked Julius if he remembered that particular discussion and how he managed to refrain from speaking profanely when the air around him was saturated by that sort of talk. He smiled as he recalled the conversation.

"The negativity of that place is so great; it's almost intoxicating. But every day I made it a point that before I went out into the day room, before I talked with anybody, I spent at least an hour either reading my Bible or reading a devotional or praying. I had this little crack of window that I could look out at the trees, the sky, the mountains. I asked for protection, for God to help me live this day as best I could for Him. The more I read the Word, the more I hid it in my heart. When I heard those words—the cursing—it was offensive to me, like someone was shouting it in my ears. I didn't want to be around it. But I never told anybody, 'Hey, don't talk like that around me.'

"There wasn't one day I didn't read my Bible. I read the Bible through five times in those two years I was locked up. There wasn't one day that I didn't read my Bible. I got a Charles Spurgeon book called *Morning and Evening*. It has a devotional, one for the morning and one for the evening. Right when I woke up, I read the devotional and it would have scriptures for the day. So I'd read those along with my own study. Then I'd pray for my family, guys on the tier, for protection. God honored those prayers. He protected my mind. I didn't allow myself to be, I guess, corrupted by that talk."

I asked if he relied on a specific scripture to help him while he was in prison.

99

Julius didn't hesitate. "Yeah, it was the very first Scripture that I ever memorized. Proverbs 3:5-6: 'Trust in the Lord with all your heart and lean not on your own understanding. In all your ways acknowledge Him and He will direct your paths.'

"I was sitting in that prison, and I knew my old life was gone, and this was my new life right now. But then I started thinking about getting out. What was I going to do, where was I going to go, what was going to happen to me? And that was the Scripture that came to my mind, Proverbs 3:5-6. I just kept repeating it to myself. I knew I didn't have to worry, that if I trusted God with everything – every thought, every emotion, every word – that He was going to direct my path. I knew it was probably not going to be the path that I thought it was going to be. It was going to be something specifically designed by Him."

As a volunteer doing Bible studies a couple times a week, I don't get to see a lot of what goes on each day inside the prison. I asked Julius if he had seen God doing things on the tier that volunteers don't get to witness.

Julius said that once he started spending more time in the dayroom, he'd bring a couple of different translations of the Bible with him and sit down at a table. Then he'd start working on a study he'd been sent. Julius said people would watch him and after a while started calling him deacon or the elder or the pastor. Then some would come to him either at the table or privately in his cell. They'd tell him that they knew he had this "God thing" going, and then say they hadn't heard from their mother or their sister in a long time. Then they'd ask him to pray for them. Julius said he'd tell them they could pray too, but they said they didn't know how to do that. So Julius would pray for them aloud so they could hear.

Julius smiled as he remembered specific instances of God showing Himself real to the inmates. "It was in those situations that I'd see God move. If we'd pray one day, then maybe within a week they'd get a letter from that person, from those people we'd just prayed about. Sometimes it was just in a day or two and they'd get a letter. And you could just see it in these guys' eyes. They'd come to my cell and say 'You will not believe what just happened! You remember that thing we were praying about, for me to hear from so and so?' they'd exclaim with big eyes.

"'Oh yeah, I remember,' I'd tell them.

"'Well, I just got a letter!'

"I could see their eyes getting misty. I'd say 'Praise God, man. I never doubted. God answers prayer. That's what He does.'

"'Thanks a lot, man,' they'd respond.

"I'd tell them, 'I didn't do anything. God's the One Who created the miracle.'"

I asked Julius if he'd ever heard any inmates actually talk of regretting their actions that landed them in prison. Not regret that they got caught, because I think we all feel that when we're caught doing something that we shouldn't. But of remorse for the pain they had caused others.

"Yeah, there were a few times, when I got to sharing about my own life, when it would happen. Usually when the door was closed and there was no one else around. I'd start sharing about my life, the regrets of my life and how I felt. It would sort of poke a hole in the dam that was built up. That 'prison face' people wear when they're around others. Then they'd start sharing about their life. And I could see it in their face, in their eyes. They'd kind of hang their head. And I knew it wasn't 'Oh darn, I got caught.' I could see that they were sincere when they were telling me that they regretted what they'd done to others. But they had to keep that prison face on when they were around the others. While we were alone they would share those things, but when we were out in the day room, it was back to the prison life."

I remembered that after Julius had served his full sentence, his release was delayed. "How much extra time did you spend past your scheduled release date?"

"It was seven months and twelve days past when I was supposed to get out." Julius gave a few details about the varying requirements from one state to another and the administrative paperwork involved. Then he talked about how he dealt with the delay. "I remember guys would ask me why I wasn't kicking the doors. I told them I didn't have to; it was out of my hands. And they'd ask what I meant. So I told them that the Bible says the Lord directs our steps. And another Scripture came to me a lot. It's in Philippians 4: 'Don't be anxious for anything, but with prayer and petition, with thanksgiving, make your request known to God. And His peace will comfort you.'

"I do remember being angry at times. I remember thinking, *God, I want to go home, and I've done my time.* But I knew the day I got out was already chosen by God. I knew that. He already knew the very day I was getting out. He knew."

I asked Julius what his biggest fear was when he got out of prison.

Julius sat up toward the edge of his chair as he clasped his hands tightly together. "What will people think of me? How will I be able to show people this new-found love I have for Christ. Can I make up for what I've done? Yeah, that was it."

He then told me about life since his release. "I still pray every day, like when I was on the inside. I pray 'God just give me one person that I can share the gospel with.' And, it doesn't happen every day. Well I'm sure there were opportunities every day, but I was like, 'You don't want me to

102

talk to *that* guy today, do You?' But the days when I was able to muster the courage to talk to somebody, it always reaped a benefit.

"At work there are some guys who are just oblivious to the Lord. In conversations they'd ask me what I believed, what do I think about space aliens or the creation of the earth. I was able to tell them that I believe God is the Creator of everything seen and unseen. I believe the world was created through Jesus. They would sit there with their mouths open and look at me. While we're working, they're watching the words they say. Some of them pulled me aside and asked me if I wasn't a Marine? I'd tell them I was and they'd say, 'But I haven't heard you curse.'

"I tell them I'm a new creation. That person that used to curse is gone; God has created something new in me. It's not that I can't curse; it's that I don't want to. I just want to try to represent Jesus as best I can. If Jesus didn't do it, then I don't want to do it."

Julius continued talking about his time at work. "I asked a guy to come to church, but he had a barrier: he was worried that people were going to talk about him. I told him that he can't worry about what people are going to say. People are always going to talk about you, if you're doing good they're going to talk about you, if you're doing bad they're going to talk about you. Just worry about what God thinks about you. Over and over the Bible says God has good thoughts toward you."

I asked Julius about a recent event at the church he was attending. The church leaders had asked people to write down something difficult that they had gone through in life for which they were thankful to God.

Julius smiled as he remembered. "At Thanksgiving they had these cards, bright yellow cards, which they asked us to fill out: giving thanks in tough times or something like that. I knew there was only one thing I could write. Only one thing that was difficult to be thankful for, tough to be thankful for. I put it in big bold print: PRISON! They put it up on the wall in the foyer along with everyone else's. It's tough to be thankful for something that caused so many people pain. Pain and heartache.

"I saw prison, not as prison, but as a hospital where God put me to get well. It's tough because I know that prison is where God fixed me. God gave me a new life. But it's tough because I heard the tears from the ones I loved. I heard them on the phone, felt them in the letters. It was tough to be thankful then."

"You've been involved with a small group of Christian believers from your church," I said. "Tell me about that."

Julius sat on the edge of his chair again. "Through small group at church, someone's brother came to visit a few weeks ago. He'd been struggling with some personal issues. After church, we all went to lunch, and we were watching football. We talked about that for a while and got into other issues. Then he asked me if I'd been in prison."

At this point, I interrupted Julius and asked how this man could have known about that.

"I think the tattoos," Julius continued, looking at his arms. "This guy asked about my experience there, in prison. I told him I was scared. I just lost everything. I thought I'd be hated once I got back to the outside. But I was looking at it through my human eyes. With my spiritual eyes, I knew God had a plan for me. If I wouldn't have gone to prison I would have continued in my sin. And if I would have died, I'd have gone to hell. He saved me by letting me go to prison. It sounds weird to say, but I think that prison was the best thing that could have happened to me.

"I was in a little cage there, and I had two choices: I could have gone one way or the other. I fell on my face and told God I knew I'd done wrong and confessed my sins to Him. Not in a conventional prayer way. I was in tears. I told God that I didn't know how to pray. I didn't know what I'm doing, I didn't know if He's even hearing this. I told Him I'm sorry for what I did and I'm asking God to help me to change the way I've been living. And I know from that moment on He started chipping away at those areas of my life. He started recreating the person that I should have been."

Julius paused a moment as he recalled more of his conversation with the man at the small group. "I'm telling him this story of how I used to struggle with alcohol and with women, and with words, movies I watched, magazines I looked at. All the things that drug me down. And he's just shaking his head as he's listening.

"Then at the next small group meeting, I got there early and saw this guy again. He told me that he'd been thinking about the things I'd told him about my life. Then he told me that my life resembled his.

"I said 'Oh man, I'm sorry, I didn't realize someone else's life could be as messed up as my life.' He said he didn't know what to do. Then people started coming to the Bible study, so I couldn't talk to him anymore right then.

"I taught the study that day. Acts 28, I think. Throughout the whole study I could see him. He didn't have a Bible, and he just had his head down. But I could see that he was listening. People were participating, and I'm asking questions and he was just sitting there.

"After the study I found out that other people in the study were praying for the guy, too. Other people told me that they felt led that they should be praying for this guy during the study. After the study, the guy said something about wishing there was more time to talk. I told him I didn't have anywhere to go right then. He said he felt like he'd done so much wrong that he couldn't be forgiven of it."

At this point in my interview with Julius, he became so emotional that he had to stop and regain his composure. After some moments, he continued relating to me what he said to the man.

"'Oh brother, that's — I felt the same way. But — if you could feel what I feel right now, you would eat those words. Because God's waiting, He's waiting to forgive you.' And I was able to open the Scriptures and I showed him 1 John 1:9: 'If you confess your sins He is faithful and just to forgive you your sins and cleanse you from all unrighteousness.' I showed him a few other Scriptures too. I said 'You know, there is no reason why your life can't start over right now. There is no reason why you can't stop living the way you're living and change the course of your life forever.'"

The man asked Julius how he could do that. "I told him that he could ask Jesus into his heart, and I asked him if he wanted to do that right now. And he said yes. Tears just started streaming down his face, he just started crying. I told him to just say this prayer as I did. So I prayed and he prayed, and he asked Jesus into his heart. Then he gave me a big old hug and said thank you. He just kept thanking me.

"I told him, 'By no means did I do anything for you. I'm just a filthy signpost on the road. Just thank God; He's the One that's doing the work. He's the One that died for you, that saved you. He's the One Who is going to give you a new life. He's the One Who has given you a new life.'

"This guy asked me the same questions that I had when I got saved. I remember he asked me, 'Is it going to get better now? Are things going to get better now?'

"'You know,' I said, 'in a way they are, but in a way, you

just stepped onto the battlefield. Now you're on God's side. We have a real enemy that is out to destroy us.'

"He said, 'What do I do?'

"I said, 'The first thing you need to do is prepare yourself for this war.' I held up the Bible and told him that this book is our sword. 'This is our weapon that we have against the enemy. You need to start reading it, putting it into your mind, into your mouth, into your heart.'

"I showed him Psalm 119:11 'I have hidden Your word in my heart that I may not sin against You.' He asked me what that meant. I told him, 'Just read the Bible, God's Word, and take it in, like taking in food for your body; this Bible is food for your soul. The more you read it, the more it's going to be in your mind. When those temptations come again, you'll have the Word of God, you'll look at both of them and you'll have a choice. This time you'll have a choice. You'll say, "Okay, this is my old way, and I can go back and drink, or I can look at the Word and say the Bible says not to be drunk." You have a choice, and the more you put it in your mind, the more you pray and ask the Holy Spirit to teach you, the better off you'll be.'

"Then I explained to him that when I was in prison I didn't have any pastors to teach me, I just sat in that cage and read the Book. I didn't know what it meant and I didn't know what it was saying, but I knew it was the Truth, and I knew that it was something that I needed to know. I just read it over and over and over again until the words were ingrained in my mind.

"I encouraged him at every opportunity he got to open the Word. Start in the book of John. Read the story of Jesus. Read through the New Testament. It's a love letter showing us that we're not the only ones who struggle. I told him the temptations he had will be there, but he didn't have to do this alone anymore. I told him that he had Jesus on his side.

"He just kept hugging me and thanking me. I told him I just happened to be in the right place at the right time. I told him of how I got to this city, how I had a dream while I was in prison that I'd be coming here even though I'd never been here before and didn't want to come here. Up until that point I was asking God, 'What am I doing in this town, why am I here?' And I told this man, 'You asking Jesus into your life made this stay in this town worth it. Forever your life is changed. Now we're going to see each other in heaven. Now you're going to spend eternity with God. I know it's difficult for you and me to wrap our minds around what eternity is, but that's a long, long time.

"Nothing in this world will ever compare to the decision that you made today. There's a party going on in heaven, and it's because of you. The Bible says that all the angels in heaven rejoice when one sinner comes to salvation.'"

With all that Julius had lived in and through, I asked him "Who is Jesus to you right now?"

He replied instantly. "Jesus is my best Friend. He's Somebody that I don't want to live without. Somebody that is always there. Somebody Who understands me. Somebody Who is quick to forgive and quick to love me. Somebody Who is quick to discipline me, but to discipline me to better me, not to punish me."

I asked Julius what's been the most difficult thing he's faced since getting out of prison.

Julius blew out a long breath. "Being away from my family. I have a son—and a daughter that I've never met. Feelings of failure, feelings that I'm not able to provide for them right now. Not being able to be with them, not being able to be what a father should be. I can't do that. I deal with that a lot. Those are the tough days."

I then asked what he found to be the best thing about being out of prison.

Julius studied on the question a while before answering. "Worship. I love worship. I love singing. The very thing I told my ex-wife I would never do. The thing I used to make fun of. Worship. I get lost in it. The music starts in a service and I close my eyes. It's different than listening to a CD or the radio. I sense God's presence. I love it."

"There are people on both sides of the razor wire," I stated, "who believe deep down that God could never forgive them for their past actions. What would you say to those people?"

"That's the furthest thing from the truth," Julius responded emphatically. "If I ever heard a lie from the enemy, that one is in bold letters. Because the *whole* reason that Jesus came to die on the cross was to offer that propitiation [appeasement] for our sins to the Father, that opportunity to be forgiven. If that was not true, then I don't think Jesus would have come to die a horrible death on the cross.

"If someone thinks they can't be forgiven, it's a lie. The enemy has blinded them to the Truth. They can't see those nail-pierced hands reaching out, and Jesus saying 'I'm right here, I'm waiting to forgive you, and I'm waiting to love you. I'm waiting for you.'"

I had learned that Julius had a family visit coming up. "I understand you're going to be going out of state soon to see your parents. What are your hopes for this visit?"

"I want to make this memorable. Every time I see them, I want it to be memorable. But what I really want is to be able to share the gospel with them. It is difficult. They know me so well. But that has always been my heartfelt desire, since I've given my heart to the Lord. I want my family to come to know the Lord. It is difficult, but I hope I can gain some ground in

109

that and share the gospel with them."

I asked Julius, "If you could do anything at all right now, what would it be?"

"I want to meet my daughter," came his solemn reply. "Meet her and hold her."

"Do you have anything else you want to share?"

"I don't think anything worth attaining should be easy. I'm thankful for God. Thankful for prison. If anyone thinks their life is hopeless, I can tell you, it's not. The Bible says we walk by faith, not by sight. We may not be able to see the road ahead; we may think it just falls over a cliff. But God sees the road He wants to put us on. Hope is a word that has been on my mind. Hope is a powerful word. God gives us hope."

* * *

It is quite understandable that victims of crimes are concerned and troubled when the system releases inmates from prison. The reality is, the vast majority of inmates will one day again walk the streets of our towns and live somewhere in our communities. When released, prisoners have many important decisions to make. From what I've seen, there is one choice that is of utmost importance. They can choose to go back to their old friends and live in the circumstances they were in before coming to prison. Or, they can leave that life behind and seek with all their hearts the One Who died on the cross for them. For, as Scripture says, "He is not far from any of us." I'm hopeful they will choose the latter.

Julius' story reminds us that there are painful consequences that can come from our bad choices in life. Yet when I hear of individuals like him, I am convinced Jesus is still in the business of seeking and saving those who are lost and making new creations out of them in the process.

There are times when it appears to me that nothing is happening within the prison Bible studies. After working all day, along with other obligations of life, I often don't feel like leaving my warm home at night and going anywhere, let alone into a prison. It is then that I remind myself that someone else once took the time and made the effort to show me the Truth and tell me about the hope found in Jesus Christ alone. When I want to stay at home, I remember that the only hope I have is the same hope that is available to these prisoners and everyone else, regardless of which side of the razor wire we live on.

At Christ's crucifixion, those were real nails driven into real hands and feet on that darkest of days. The message of Jesus' cross, His substitutionary sacrifice on that cross, taking the hell I deserve for my sins and giving me His righteousness in exchange, is overflowing with hope. The hope of someday spending eternity in heaven with Him, along with walking with Him daily right now by the promised Holy Spirit, is real. This message of the cross, along with Christ's glorious resurrection from the dead, is a remarkable message someone once explained to me and showed me in the Bible. As I put my faith in Jesus the Christ, I realized the reality of His forgiveness and the reality of becoming a new creation in spite of myself. By giving His Son Jesus to shed His precious blood and die for us, God has given us all a chance. He did that by providing a way when there was no way we could get there on our own. God truly has given us hope.

Trust in the LORD with all your heart, And lean not on your own understanding; In all your ways acknowledge

Him, And He shall direct your paths. Do not be wise in your own eyes; Fear the LORD and depart from evil. It will be health to your flesh, And strength to your bones (Proverbs 3:5-8).

May the God of hope fill you with all joy and peace as you trust in him, so that you may overflow with hope by the power of the Holy Spirit (Romans 15:13 NIV).

All honor to the God and Father of our Lord Jesus Christ, for it is by his boundless mercy that God has given us the privilege of being born again. Now we live with a wonderful expectation because Jesus Christ rose again from the dead (1 Peter 1:3 NLT).

God did this so that men would seek him and perhaps reach out for him and find him, though he is not far from each one of us (Acts 17:27 NIV).

The LORD takes pleasure in those who fear Him, In those who hope in His mercy (Psalm 147:11).

For "Anyone who calls on the name of the Lord will be saved." But how can they call on him to save them unless they believe in him? And how can they believe in him if they have never heard about him? And how can they hear about him unless someone tells them? And how will anyone go and tell them without being sent? That is what the Scriptures mean when they say, "How beautiful are the feet of those who bring good news!" But not everyone welcomes the Good News, for Isaiah the prophet said, "Lord, who has believed our message?" Yet faith comes from listening to this message of good news—the Good News about Christ (Romans 10:13-17 NLT).

For by grace you have been saved through faith, and that not of yourselves; it is the gift of God, not of works, lest anyone should boast. For we are His workmanship, created in Christ Jesus for good works, which God prepared beforehand that we should walk in them. Therefore remember that you, once Gentiles in the flesh—who are called Uncircumcision by what is called the Circumcision made in the flesh by hands—that at that time you were without Christ, being aliens from the commonwealth of Israel and strangers from the covenants of promise, having no hope and without God in the world. But now in Christ Jesus you who once were far off have been brought near by the blood of Christ (Ephesians 2:8-13).

For He made Him who knew no sin to be sin for us, that we might become the righteousness of God in Him (2 Corinthians 5:21).

Jesus said to him, "I am the way, the truth, and the life. No one comes to the Father except through Me (John 14:6).

Jesus Christ is the same yesterday, today, and forever (Hebrews 13:8).

Time continues to tick away for us all. Jesus hasn't changed, and He continues to hold out His free gift of forgiveness and salvation to you right now, right where you are, and just as you are. However, Jesus also promised to come back for those who have made Him Lord and Savior of their lives, and to take them home to be with Him in heaven forever.

None of us on earth knows when that moment will be or when we will take our last breath. When either time comes, our chance to call on Him for forgiveness will be gone forever.

Scripture tells us that we are destined to die once and then face judgment (Hebrews 9:27). If you have never called out to Jesus, the One Who died for your sins on that cross, I urge you with every fiber of my being not to delay in your decision for Him. The gift of salvation is free, but it is not cheap. God gave His only Son to die a horrific death to pay the penalty for our sins.

Accepting or rejecting Jesus is the most important decision you and I will ever make in life. If you desire to receive this gift, you can pray this prayer or pray in your own words. Your heart is important to God:

Dear God, I am a sinner. I confess this to You right now, and I take full responsibility for my sins. I confess to You all the addictions, all the lies, every wrong I've ever done. I confess to you my sins and I repent of them, turn away from them, and turn to You. I believe that Your Son Jesus died on the cross and shed His blood to pay for my sins and I believe He rose again on the third day. I ask You, Jesus, to forgive me of my sins and be the Lord and Savior of my life, now and forever. Thank You for hearing me, forgiving me, and accepting me. Guide me now by Your precious Holy Spirit. Thank You, God.

All whom My Father gives (entrusts) to Me will come to Me; and the one who comes to Me I will most certainly not cast out [I will never, no never, reject one of them who comes to Me]. (John 6:37 AMP).

For more information please visit:

Thomastrock.com

Made in the USA
Middletown, DE
30 June 2018